LFC
JK
AXA

LIVERPOOL

THE JÜRGEN KLOPP YEARS

WRITTEN BY IAIN SPRAGG

sona BOOKS

sona BOOKS

First published in the UK by Sona Books, an imprint of Danann Media Publishing Limited

CAT NO: SON0614

Photography courtesy of

Getty images, Alamy and Wiki Commons

Project editor: Martin Corteel

Book layout & design: Kevin Gardner

Proofreader: Cameron Thurlow

Made in EU.

ISBN: 978-1-917259-01-9

CONTENTS

INTRODUCTION

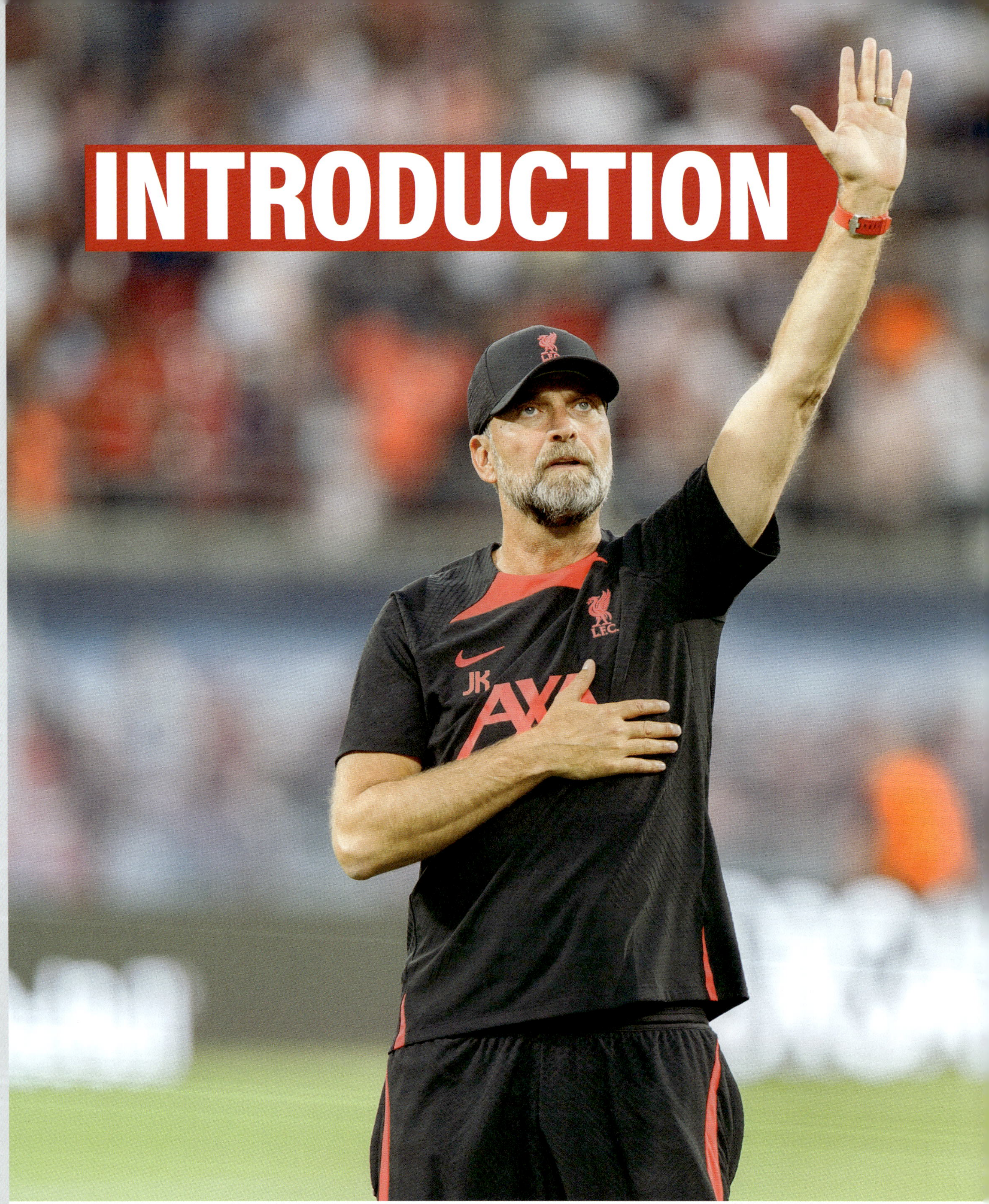

Only the late, great Bob Paisley lifted more trophies with the Reds than Klopp.

A manager blessed with natural talent and charisma in equal measure, Jürgen Klopp's remarkable reign at Liverpool was one during which a great club rediscovered its soul and proudly revelled in Merseyside's reputation as a Mecca of the beautiful game. The German's impact on the club was truly transformational, as well as trophy laden, and he stands undisputed as the Reds' greatest manager of the 21st century.

When he arrived in England in October 2015, few could have predicted what Klopp would achieve in his nine glittering years on Merseyside. His infectious personality, unwavering belief in entertaining football and his instant affinity with the fans ensured he quickly became part of the club's DNA and his team responded on the pitch to create one of the most successful eras in Liverpool's long and illustrious history.

Only the late, great Bob Paisley lifted more trophies with the Reds than Klopp. His triumph in the 2019 Champions League final, the German's first silverware for the club, reignited memories of the club's many fabled European nights but even the party that erupted in Madrid after victory was eclipsed by the celebrations when Liverpool were crowned champions of England a year later. The 30-year wait for the title was over and Klopp was the man who had finally erased three decades of hurt.

Seven major trophies saw Klopp complete the clean sweep of domestic honours, while Liverpool's maiden victory in the FIFA Club World Cup in 2019 reaffirmed the club's status as one of the few of the global game's genuine heavyweights.

Patrolling the Anfield touchline with a raw energy invariably accompanied by a broad smile, Klopp was a footballing force of nature whose tactical acumen was as pivotal to the Reds' success as his ability to connect with his side and the crowd. Nothing the larger-than-life German did on Merseyside was affected and his players and the Anfield faithful loved him for it.

SEEDS OF SUCCESS (2015-16)

Only the 21st manager in Liverpool's long and illustrious history, Jürgen Klopp arrived at Anfield in 2015 vowing to deliver his trademark brand of 'heavy metal' football.

When Klopp faced the British media for the first time in early October, the 48-year-old German was predictably bombarded with questions about the managerial greats who had preceded him at Anfield. Following in the iconic footsteps of Bill Shankly, Bob Paisley and Kenny Dalglish may have understandably daunted less confident coaches but Klopp was adamant he would not be overwhelmed by the famous weight of expectation on the red half of Merseyside.

"I'm a normal guy from the Black Forest," he told the reporters who'd eagerly assembled to interrogate him, demonstrating the modesty that would quickly become one of his most endearing trademarks. "I don't compare myself to these genius managers in the history of Liverpool. Not one of these great managers said in his first press conference that his target was to be a legend at the end, so I don't

"This is now the perfect next step for me. It's the biggest honour I can imagine."

think about it. The people live football in Liverpool, around Liverpool, all Liverpool fans all over the world. It's not a normal club, it's a special club. This is now a perfect next step for me. It's the biggest honour I can imagine."

Nine years after his arrival in the city, Klopp's place in the pantheon of the club's greatest managers was assured. His rebuild at Anfield was an astute and patient one but once the German had secured the first silverware of his reign, nothing less than the Champions League trophy itself in 2019, his unfolding Liverpool story was to bring repeated success and entertainment. Klopp catapulted the Reds back

RIGHT: **The centre of attention, Klopp is all smiles at his Liverpool unveiling alongside CEO Ian Ayre (left) and Chairman Tom Werner (right).**

He began his career as a striker, then was later redeployed in defence, but in 2001 at the age of 33 he hung up his boots.

to the pinnacle of domestic, European and world football and the platform was laid by the irrepressible German during his first season in the dugout.

A NEW ERA

It was just an hour after Liverpool's frustrating 1-1 draw with Everton at Goodison Park that the club announced Brendan Rodgers had been sacked as manager after three-and-a-half years in charge. It later emerged that the Reds had taken the difficult decision to dispense with the Northern Irishman's services before kick-off and although Rodgers had taken the team agonisingly close to the Premier League title in 2013-14, Liverpool were now languishing in 10th in the table after eight games with only 12 points on the board and the Anfield faithful accepted the time had come for change. Four days later Klopp flew into John Lennon Airport on a private jet and was announced as Rodgers' replacement.

By his own admission he had been no more than a journeyman player during his 11 years with Mainz 05 in the second tier of German football, despite making over 300 appearances for the club. He began his career as a striker, then was later redeployed in defence, but in 2001 at the age of 33 he hung up his boots. Klopp knew that the touchline rather than out on the pitch was where he would shine and while still playing, absorbed as much information and as many ideas as possible from his Mainz's coaches and managers.

The club recognised his as yet unproven potential and he began his managerial apprenticeship with Mainz at the start of the 2001-02 season. After three years at the helm in the German second-tier, Klopp masterminded the club's promotion to the Bundesliga in 2004 for the first time in their history but having taken the club as far as he believed he could, three years later he stepped down.

ABOVE: Klopp cuts a casual figure as manager of Mainz. On his left are Stephan Kuhnert and Željko Buvač.

OPPOSITE: Collecting his thoughts whilst in charge of the German team Borussia Dortmund.

A self-imposed year out of the game followed until Borussia Dortmund came calling in the summer of 2008. The job was a clear step up for him despite his achievements with Mainz but he decisively dispelled any doubts he could cope with the pressure of managing one of German football's biggest beasts. Klopp won five major trophies with the club and his greatest success was dethroning Bayern

A self-imposed year out of the game followed until Borussia Dortmund came calling in the summer of 2008.

Munich as champions when Dortmund claimed the 2010-11 Bundesliga title. They defended their domestic crown the following year and although there was last-gasp heartbreak in the 2013 Champions League final, losing 2-1 to Bayern in the 89th minute at Wembley, Klopp had already built a reputation as one of Europe's most innovative and influential managers.

As he had done at Mainz however, Klopp decided to leave Dortmund on his own terms when he revealed in April 2015 he would not manage the team the following season and quit at the end of the campaign after seven years, earning him the distinction as the club's longest-serving manager. During his tenure, Klopp was twice voted the Manager of the Year in Germany. His voluntary, four-month-long sabbatical afforded him the opportunity to take

his family on an extended holiday but when Liverpool made their move, offering the German a three-year deal worth £15 million, he needed no persuasion to sign the contract.

His first press conference the day following news of his appointment came after just one meeting with the Liverpool squad but despite his unfamiliarity with the players, Klopp was in no doubt what he expected from them and how the Reds under his new leadership would be expected set out their stall.

"We must turn from doubters to believers," he told the packed media room. "Everyone knows me, it's about emotion, it's about speed. All the things that make football interesting for me I want to see on the pitch. I said [I wanted to play] full throttle football in Dortmund but my God I cannot always say the same things. But it will be full throttle football. It's really important that the player feels the difference. They have to think they can reach the expectations of the fans, of the press. We have to start together new and then we will see what will happen this year. We have to change performance of course because nobody is satisfied in this moment.

"Sometimes you are not satisfied because you do not see the big steps in developments you wait for, because of the money they spend. Don't think about money, only think about football. If you want to enjoy the game you have to be prepared for this. You have to come to the stadium to see something. Fighting spirit, sprinting, lots of shots, all these things. It's the biggest honour I can imagine, for me at one of the biggest clubs in the world."

As for Klopp's penchant for 'heavy metal' football, a phrase he coined himself and underlined his belief in dynamic counter-attacking and a relentless hunt for the ball, it was a legacy of his time at Dortmund

ABOVE: Facing the music, Klopp meets the media at his first press conference.

OPPOSITE: Liverpool visited Tottenham for Klopp's entry into Premiership management.

"We must turn from doubters to believers."

and in particular a 2013 Champions League clash with Arsenal. "I think he [Gunners manager Arsène Wenger] likes having the ball, playing football, passes, it's like an orchestra," he had said in the build-up to the match. "But it's a silent song. I like heavy metal more. I always want it loud."

CAPTAIN'S FAREWELL

Liverpool fans had witnessed a relatively busy transfer window in the summer of 2015 under Rodgers before Klopp's move to Merseyside. Joe Gomez, James Milner, Roberto Firmino and Christian Benteke were among the eight recruits to join the Reds family while Glen Johnson and, controversially, Raheem Sterling both left Anfield for new challenges.

The deals paled in significance however compared to the sense of loss when Steven Gerrard said goodbye to the Reds that summer. After over 700 appearances, eight trophies and 17 glittering seasons at Anfield, the last 12 of them as club captain, Gerrard had been the heartbeat of the team for so long that it was difficult to envisage a future without the 35-year-old as he jetted over the Atlantic to sign for LA Galaxy and a brief adventure in the MLS. Rodgers turned to fellow midfielder Jordan Henderson to become Anfield's new leader and it was a decision that Klopp wisely saw no reason to reverse when he became manager.

The German's first game at the helm was a trip to North London to face Spurs at White Hart Lane in mid-October. There were no seismic shocks in Klopp's selection for the fixture, less than two weeks after his appointment, and although a goalless draw in the capital was hardly cause for wild celebrations, there were clear positives. Simon Mignolet was undeniably the busier of the two goalkeepers on the day but the clean sheet was only Liverpool's second in the

league while the energy from his players was very much in evidence. During the Tottenham clash the Reds collectively covered 116km over the 90 minutes to earn their point, more than in any of their previous eight Premier League outings. It was also the first time that season that the home side had been outrun by the opposition. Klopp's vision of injecting real pace and relentless movement into the team on and off the ball was already beginning to take shape.

"The nil on the right side is OK, the nil on the other side doesn't give you the same feeling," he said after the game. I am happy because I saw many good things. In the first 20 minutes we were pressing and were very aggressive. We will get stronger. We were a little bit nervous when we got the ball because the pulse was a little too high at this moment. There were many full-throttle moments in the game. We need to improve but after working with the players for three days, I am completely satisfied."

The first goal of the Klopp era came five days later courtesy of a first-half Emre Can strike against Russian side Rubin Kazan in the Europa League while his first victory was at the end of October when the Reds beat Bournemouth at Anfield in the League Cup. Nathaniel Clyne scored the only goal of the Round Four encounter, his first for the club, and Klopp was up and running.

For the remainder of the league campaign consistency – and consecutive wins – proved elusive. Only once did Liverpool register three back-to-back victories but there were nonetheless significant highlights as the German began, albeit gradually, to mould the side in his own, crowd-pleasing image. Home and away triumphs over Manchester City with an aggregate scoreline of 7-1 gave the faithful cause for considerable optimism and while the first Merseyside derby of the season had brought down the curtain on Rodgers' Liverpool career, Klopp's first

taste of the fixture in April was an altogether more uplifting experience for the new manager as his team dismantled the Toffees at Anfield and roared to a 4-0 win.

An eventual eighth-place finish in the Premier League was of course far from stellar for a club with perennial ambitions to be champions but Klopp's emerging Reds hinted at what was to come with confident displays in both the League Cup and Europa League, only narrowly failing to deliver a trophy on both fronts in his debut campaign.

TWO FINALS, DOUBLE HEARTBREAK

Before 2015-16 Liverpool had not progressed to a major knockout final, either domestic or European, for three frustrating seasons. It was the club's longest

ABOVE: Emre Can scores for Liverpool against Rubin Kazan.

absence from a showpiece fixture for more than a decade and although Klopp was not blessed with time to prepare his troops for the fray, his Reds shone brightly regardless as they marched into the League Cup and then Europa League finals.

Their tilt at domestic glory was ignited by a 6-1 demolition of Southampton in January 2016 in the last eight of the League Cup and a hat-trick from Divock Origi. Victory booked their place in the semi-finals against Stoke City and although the two legs saw the sides deadlocked 1-1 after extra time in the second game at Anfield, Mignolet saved twice in the resulting lottery of a penalty shootout and Liverpool were through.

Wembley had proved a happy hunting ground for the Reds on their last visit – a shootout triumph over Swansea City in the League Cup in 2012 – but four years on they were left cursing rather than praising their luck from the penalty spot in London. Manchester City were their opponents this time and leading 1-0, were on course for victory inside normal time before Philippe Coutinho levelled with only sevens minutes left.

A shootout demands heroes and villains and while it was Mignolet who took the plaudits in the semi-finals, it was his opposite number Willy Caballero who made the headlines for City at the home of football with pivotal saves from Lucas, Coutinho and Adam Lallana. Klopp's dream of glory in his first Liverpool season had been cruelly snatched away.

"We feel down but now we have to stand up."

"We feel down but now we have to stand up," he said with his characteristic mixture of honesty and passion. "Only silly idiots stay on the floor and wait for the next defeat. We will strike back. We have felt how it is to lose. It is not the best moment but on Monday morning maybe we can change everything. We will go on and we will get better. We have to work really hard, carry on and there is light at the end of the tunnel."

The Europa League challenge offered the chance of knockout redemption and a first European final since 2007. The group phase of the competition was two games old – both disappointing draws against Bordeaux and FC Sion – before Klopp was installed and once he had taken charge, the team's continental fortunes improved significantly and they progressed to the Last 32 as group winners. The side's 1-0 aggregate win over German side Augsburg was little to write home about, but the latter stages of the tournament served up undiluted drama.

Old and fiercest of foes Manchester United lay in wait in the next round. Anfield hosted the first leg in March, which was won 2-0 thanks to goals from Daniel Sturridge and Roberto Firmino and although a first-half score at Old Trafford gave United brief hope of overturning the deficit, Coutinho's goal snubbed out the danger of a recovery and Liverpool progressed safely to the last eight.

Klopp's old club Dortmund stood in his way in an emotional if unexpectedly early reunion with

his former employers. Liverpool marked the 27th anniversary of the Hillsborough disaster with a minute's silence before kick-off at Anfield in the second leg and with the tie tantalisingly poised at 1-1 after the first game in Germany, there was a palpable sense of both anticipation and nervousness in the stadium. To the initial dismay of the Kop, the visitors stormed into a 3-1 lead but Coutinho and Mamadou Sakho pegged them back, setting the stage for Dejan Lovren to complete the pure theatre as he leapt highest in the box in the first minute of stoppage time to head home the winner. The result was one of the greatest comebacks in any competition in the club's remarkable history.

There was, perhaps mercifully, less drama in the semi-final victory over Villarreal, a 3-1 aggregate success. Fellow Spanish club Sevilla were the last hurdle for Liverpool in the final staged at the St.

LEFT: Klopp stands shoulder to shoulder with his team, before facing Manchester City at Wembley in the League Cup final.

BELOW: Liverpool and Manchester United walk out ahead of their UEFA Europa League match.

Jakob-Park in the Swiss city of Basel in May but despite Liverpool's growing sense of identity and resilience under Klopp, the La Liga side went into the match as favourites having lifted the Europa League trophy in the two previous seasons. A sublime 35th-minute strike from Sturridge, the striker curling the ball in with the outside of his left foot from the angle of the area, sent the travelling Liverpool support wild but Sevilla were not to be denied and three second-half goals gave them the silverware for a third successive year.

It may not have been the fairy-tale climax to his first, albeit shortened campaign for the German but the reaction from seasoned observers of the Reds over the years was overwhelmingly positive despite the agonising near misses.

"Klopp's first seven months in charge at Liverpool sped by," the *Liverpool Echo* wrote. "Full throttle, he called it, at his unveiling in October. How right he was. Thirty-nine players, 52 games, 104 press conferences, two finals. Klopp arrived at a club whose direction was unclear. On the field, there was no defined style of play: a collective of individuals, rather than a team. Off the field, it was just as unclear.

"Enter the German. He came with a reputation of playing a certain style of football, and a clear identity off the field too. Liverpool would now be a club that looks to nurture top talent with a high-intensity, complex pressing game. The German has been with the club less than a year, but statements are already being made – the vast majority of them in favour, in truth.

"Enter the German. He came with a reputation of playing a certain style of football, and a clear identity off the field too."

"Rightly so. The improvement at Anfield since his arrival is evident. The Reds needed a change after Brendan Rodgers lost both the fans' belief and his own. Klopp was a blockbuster acquisition, a no-brainer of an appointment to excite, unite, and begin what [the owners] FSG hopes is the club's ascension back to the top. While Rodgers had lost the crowd by the end of his tenure, Klopp had found them. While Rodgers had lost sight of what he wanted to do at Anfield, Klopp came with a clear vision. In less than a season, the implementation of that has begun. There is no question how the Reds, and Klopp, plan to achieve success – it is now about whether they can carry it out."

ABOVE: Jürgen Klopp and the Liverpool side show their appreciation of the crowd at Anfield.

OPPOSITE: Nathaniel Clyne of Liverpool tussles with Sergio Escudero of Sevilla.

ROAD BACK TO EUROPE (2016-17)

After a first preseason, Jürgen Klopp set his sights on the first phase of his ambitious Anfield overhaul and the chance to lay down a marker to Liverpool's rivals.

Once the dust had settled on Klopp's encouraging debut campaign, attention inevitably turned to what he might achieve the following season. The failure of the side to make an impression on the title race, or qualify for Europe in 2015-16, was forgivable given his belated arrival in the city, but the German was under no illusions that neither the supporters nor the club hierarchy would not be as understanding a second time if Liverpool stood still for another season. Tangible progress was paramount.

If Klopp was feeling any pressure, the weight of expectation was significantly lightened in July 2016 when the club announced they had extended their manager's contract. He had signed his initial deal, which ran until 2018, only 10 months earlier but Liverpool were already convinced he was the man to build a lasting legacy on Merseyside and Klopp was handed improved terms committing him to the Reds until 2022. It was a resounding vote of confidence which would enable the German to accelerate his long-term plans for reshaping the team.

"His leadership will be critical to everything we hope to achieve," the club said when the new contract was made public. "The ideas and plans he has for the football infrastructure excite us. We believe it benefits the organisation to have Jürgen

Crucially the club's contractual backing also extended to Željko Buvač and Peter Krawietz, Klopp's assistant managers and most trusted lieutenants.

committed to Liverpool for a sustained period, to make sure he is here to oversee this development. When you have an individual of Jürgen's quality in the building it makes perfect sense to secure that person for the long term. To not do so would be irresponsible."

Crucially the club's contractual backing also extended to Željko Buvač and Peter Krawietz, Klopp's assistant managers and most trusted lieutenants who he had drafted into the Reds' coaching set-up back in October. Klopp had made it clear in 2015 he could only accept the Liverpool job if he was flanked on the touchline by the two men he had collaborated with so successfully first at Mainz and subsequently Dortmund and his faith in them to help deliver his project at Anfield was reflected in improved contracts from the club for both.

The eldest of the coaching trio, Buvač met Klopp after spending three seasons in the same Mainz side in the 1990s and was recruited by his former team-mate when he was named manager in 2001. Klopp dubbed the Bosnian-Serb 'The Brain' in recognition of his tactical expertise. Fellow German Krawietz was Mainz's chief scout before joining Klopp in the dugout

ABOVE: Klopp with his dependable aides, Željko Buvač and Peter Krawietz at a Liverpool training session, Melwood.

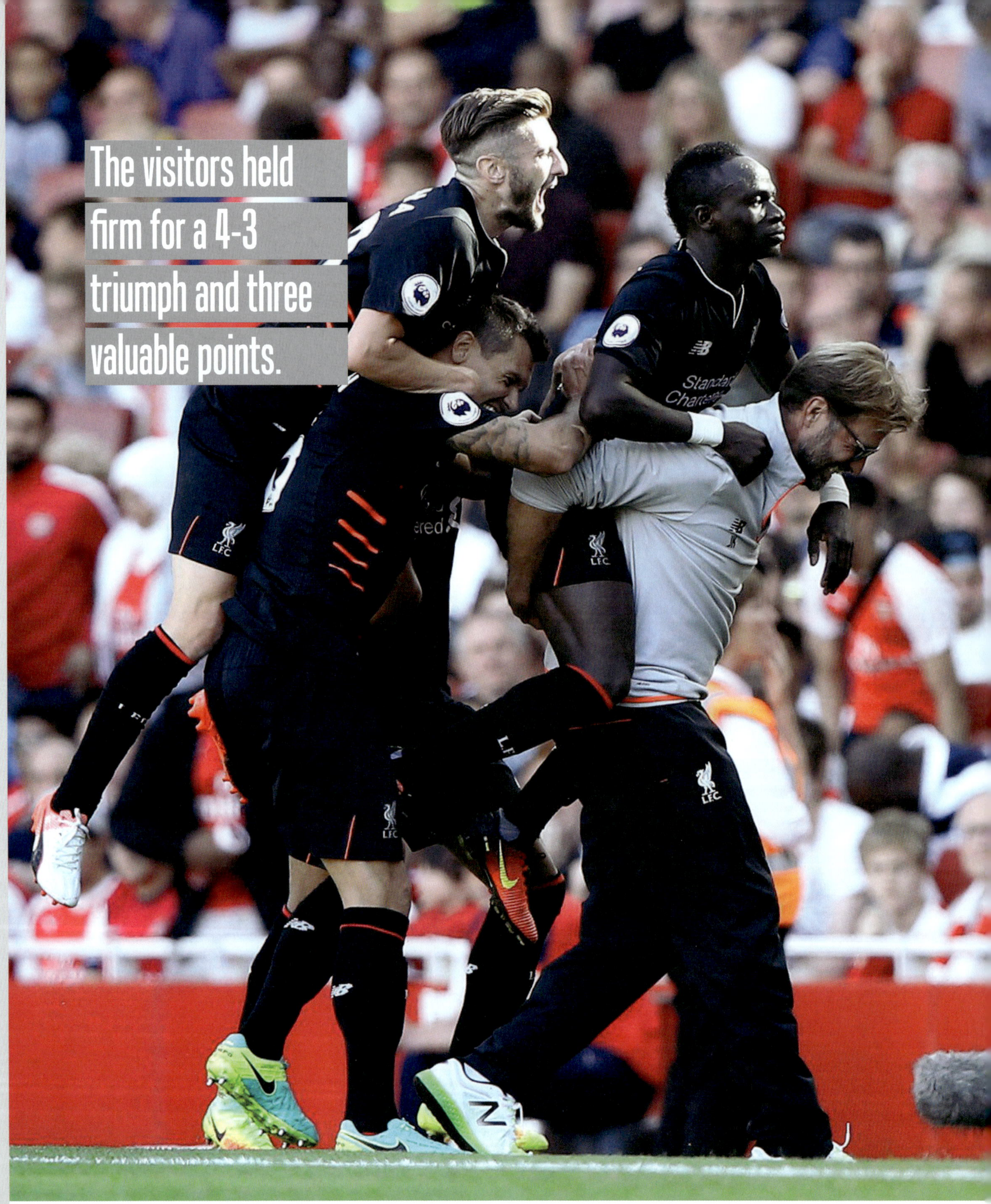

The visitors held firm for a 4-3 triumph and three valuable points.

and 'The Eye', as Klopp nicknamed him, quickly established a reputation for his analytical skills.

With Liverpool's coaching structure reaffirmed, Klopp could now focus on his first summer transfer window on Merseyside. He sanctioned the transfer or release of 14 players in total, most notably the defensive trio of Kolo Touré, Martin Škrtel and José Enrique and striker Christian Benteke, but it was the signing of Sadio Mané from Southampton that was to prove his most significant piece of business. At £36 million the Senegalese forward was not by modern standards an unduly expensive addition to the squad, while his early career in France, Austria and England had so far been solid rather than spectacular, but Klopp had seen something others had not in Mané and the player would go on to vindicate his manager over his following six seasons in red in prolific style.

ANTICIPATION, AWARDS AND ARSENAL

The 2016-17 season marked Liverpool's 125th anniversary since its formation in 1892. It was also, proudly, their 55th consecutive campaign in the English top flight and as one of only six surviving clubs from the inaugural Premier League of 1992-93, it was a 25th successive term at the top table of domestic football.

A season of such notable milestones deserved, perhaps demanded, a positive start and Klopp's players delivered in August with a pulsating 4-3 win over Arsenal at the Emirates. Liverpool hadn't won on the road against the Gunners, runners-up in the league in 2015-16, for five years but a seven-goal thriller in North London brought an explosive end to the sequence. The home side went in front on the half hour but the goal merely sparked Klopp's team into life and they replied with an unanswered four-goal salvo either side of the break. The fourth goal was claimed by Mané with a fierce finish, a score which was celebrated by the new signing on debut jumping joyously on the German's back and although two more Arsenal goals made the closing minutes more nervous than they should have been, the visitors held firm for a 4-3 triumph and three valuable points. Klopp later admitted it was a mistake to celebrate with his players before the three points had been safely secured at the Emirates but from the fans' perspective, there were no complaints about one of his earliest outpourings of unfiltered emotion on the touchline.

Defeat to Burnley at Turf Moor six days later was not in the script but September saw the Reds hit a purple patch in the league. Defending champions Leicester, Chelsea and Hull City were all despatched in the space of a fortnight for nine points from nine and when the Premier League Manager of the Month was announced, it was no surprise that Klopp was the recipient of the award for the first time. He became the first German coach to receive the accolade and in the process denied fellow nominee Pep Guardiola, newly arrived in England with Manchester City, the gong. It was a foretaste of the intense rivalry that would develop between two managers separated by a mere 35 miles in the North West.

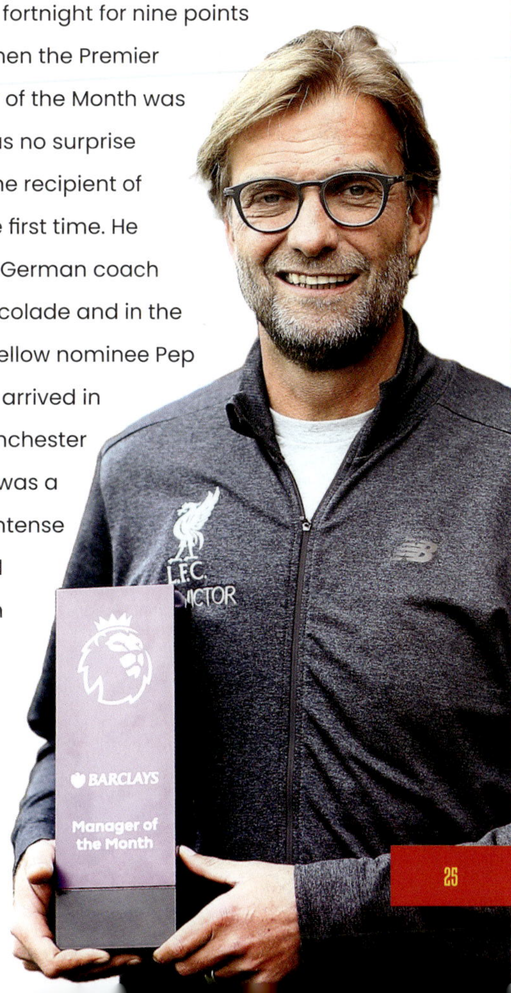

OPPOSITE: A moment of joy for Mané, as he celebrates his goal against Arsenal in style, leaping on his managers back.

RIGHT: Klopp poses for the camera with the Manager of the Month award.

"I went into the office of my coaches and said, 'we are Manager of the Month,'" Klopp revealed after picking up the award, offering a deliberate insight

> "I went into the office of my coaches and said, 'we are Manager of the Month.'"

to the collective culture he was nurturing at Anfield. "I don't need personal prizes. We are on a good way but there are so many good teams in this division and so many difficult games for us which we have to be ready for. I'm fine with the moment but we have to play more games and hopefully we perform well."

His squad listened attentively to their manager's message and strung together a seven-match unbeaten run which finally came to an end in early December. The results took Liverpool up to second in the table, a single point behind Chelsea, but they were unable to maintain the momentum in the New Year and as the league season neared its climax a top-four finish was far from guaranteed. A 4-0 away rout of West Ham in their penultimate fixture took the Reds into third and a 3-0 win over Middlesbrough at Anfield on the last day secured fourth place and qualification for the Champions League play-offs, ahead of both Arsenal and Manchester United.

The dream of seriously challenging for the title may have dimmed in the second half of the campaign but there was still much to admire in Klopp's side's efforts. Reaching the Champions League was only the second time in eight years the club had gained entry to Europe's marquee competition while their haul of 76 points was a significant improvement on the previous two seasons. Ultimately the Reds finished four places and 16 points better off than they had in 2015-16.

Significantly the manager appeared to be getting to grips with Liverpool's defensive weaknesses, a fragility that many believed was their most pressing problem. The 42 league goals conceded in 2016-17 represented their most miserly season-long performance for five years. There were also signs that

Significantly the manager appeared to be getting to grips with Liverpool's defensive weaknesses.

Klopp was increasingly clear about the make-up of his squad and used only 23 players in the Premier League, the joint lowest number in the division.

"To finish in the top four Klopp has done very well and he'll be happy, especially going from seventh to pushing for the title at one point," Reds legend Phil Thompson, a seven-time league champion and three-time European Cup winner with the club in the 1970s and '80s, told *Sky Sports*. "However, on the flip side of that, to have not finished in the top four would have made it a poor season from the high of New Year's Eve [beating Manchester City at Anfield]. But without much net spend he's done an excellent job, so I'm really looking forward to the summer.

"The [transfer] targets are a centre-back, left-back and a more controlling midfield player. I think next season, with the right acquisitions, we'll have ambitions of winning the title, the same as the rest of the top six. It will be difficult, especially with European football, so it will certainly be interesting, but they should be able to compete. In terms of Champions League hopes, I would think, because we haven't been consistently in the competition, quarter-finals would be the right target."

OPPOSITE: **Philippe Coutinho scores for Liverpool in their match with Hull City at Anfield, September 2016.**

BELOW: **Liverpool's Nathaniel Clyne controls the ball from Callum Wilson of AFC Bournemouth, December 2016.**

Predictions of respectability in reaching the last eight in Europe however would happily prove wide of the mark.

FATHER FIGURE

With Klopp's focus firmly on reviving the club's league fortunes, it was inevitable that the side's displays in the cup competitions would be secondary to the manager. Two final appearances in his first season had exceeded expectations and in 2016-17 injuries, international duty, pragmatism and an eagerness to expose his fringe players to first team football dictated that he select a series of relatively unfamiliar starting XIs in both domestic competitions.

Their FA Cup adventure was over almost as soon as it started. Drawn against League One side Plymouth Argyle in the third round in early January, the Reds stuttered against their lower league opposition at Anfield and after a goalless draw on Merseyside, they were forced to make the trip to Devon for a replay 10 days later. Liverpool found the rematch no easier and blushes were only spared from the unlikeliest of sources, Brazilian midfielder Lucas Leiva. His first-half goal, the only score of the game, was his first in seven years.

At the end of the month they welcomed Wolverhampton Wanderers to Merseyside in the next round. The Championship club scored after only 53 seconds and went two in front before half-time while Divock Origi's late score was no more than a consolation rather than the catalyst for a glorious last-gasp fight back. The FA Cup was over for the Reds less than three weeks after it had begun.

There was though more for Klopp and the fans to savour in the League Cup. Liverpool reached the semi-finals but arguably the most satisfying element of the competition, in terms of the manager's rebuild and the momentum it was gathering, was the fourth round clash with Spurs at Anfield in October. Once again the German's team was far from the strongest he could have fielded but the fixture gave him the chance to hand a debut to a young defender by the name of Trent Alexander-Arnold.

Only recently turned 18, the teenager was only the 18th Liverpool-born player to break into the first team since Steven Gerrard had joined the senior ranks back in 1998 and while Klopp's decision was of course popular with the supporters, the promotion of a player who had been associated with the club since the age of six was not designed to please the crowd. Klopp would blood many graduates of the Reds' Academy during his nine seasons on Merseyside and the selection of Trent Alexander-Arnold was proof he had both the eye to identify a true star in the making and the courage to pick them. Despite being booked at Anfield before he was substituted in the 68th minute, the right-back didn't put a foot wrong in the 2-1 Reds' victory and thanks to the faith shown by his manager, the youngster was on his way to realising his stellar potential for club and, less than two years later, representing his country at the World Cup.

"I have known Trent Alexander-Arnold since he was 17 years old," Klopp said after the Spurs game, singling out his mental strength for particular praise. "He had power for around 60 minutes, he was a big talent but we were not sure he could do it

"I have known Trent Alexander-Arnold since he was 17 years old."

physically. You need to come back into a game when you have difficult moments, like the yellow card. He stayed in the game and made a lot of challenges against the winger and to do it smartly, that's a really good sign."

The player himself was clear what Klopp's vote of confidence meant and, under the patient guidance of the German, he seized his big chance decisively.

"He's been a massive influence," Alexander-Arnold said in 2018. "You hear a lot of players saying

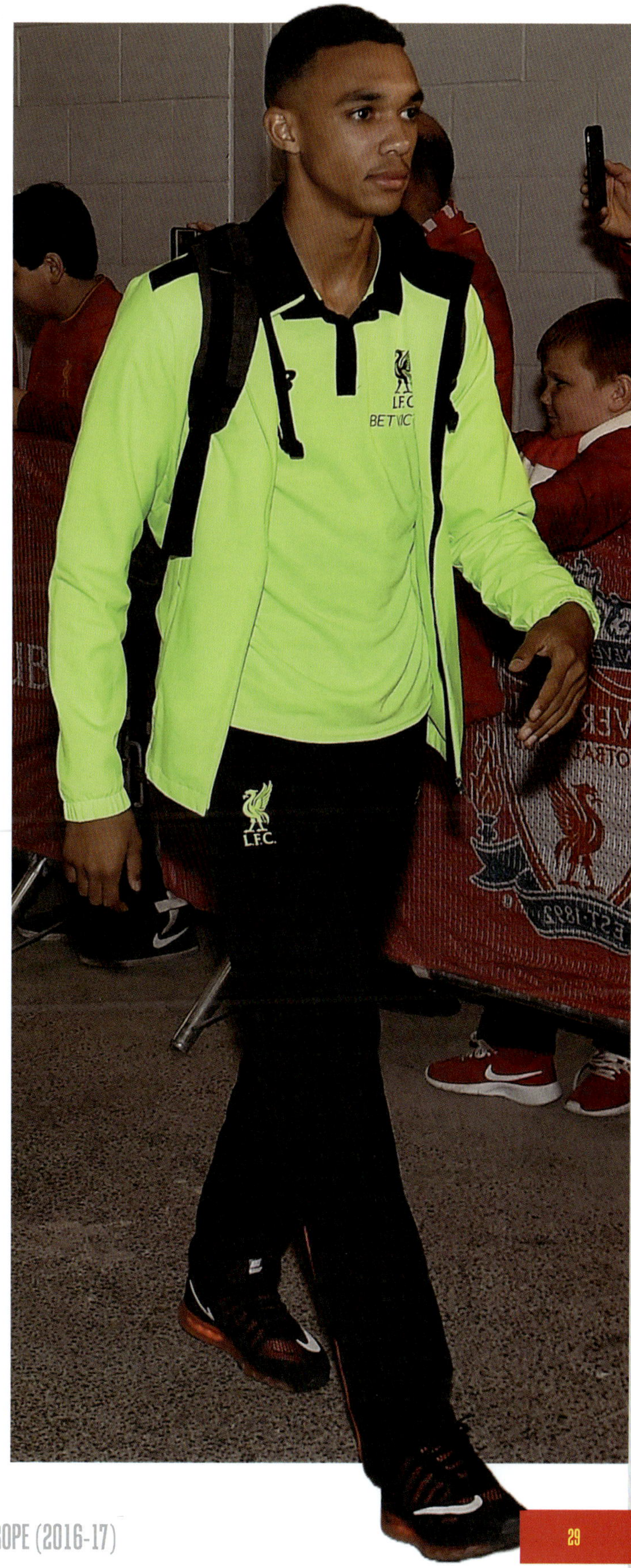

OPPOSITE: Georginio Wijnaldum hugs Klopp after Liverpool's victory over Manchester City at Anfield, December 2016.

RIGHT: Jürgen Klopp was keen to bring in seasoned Liverpool youngsters, among them Trent Alexander-Arnold.

"He understands the game unbelievably well."

"He knows what to say, when to say it and how to say it."

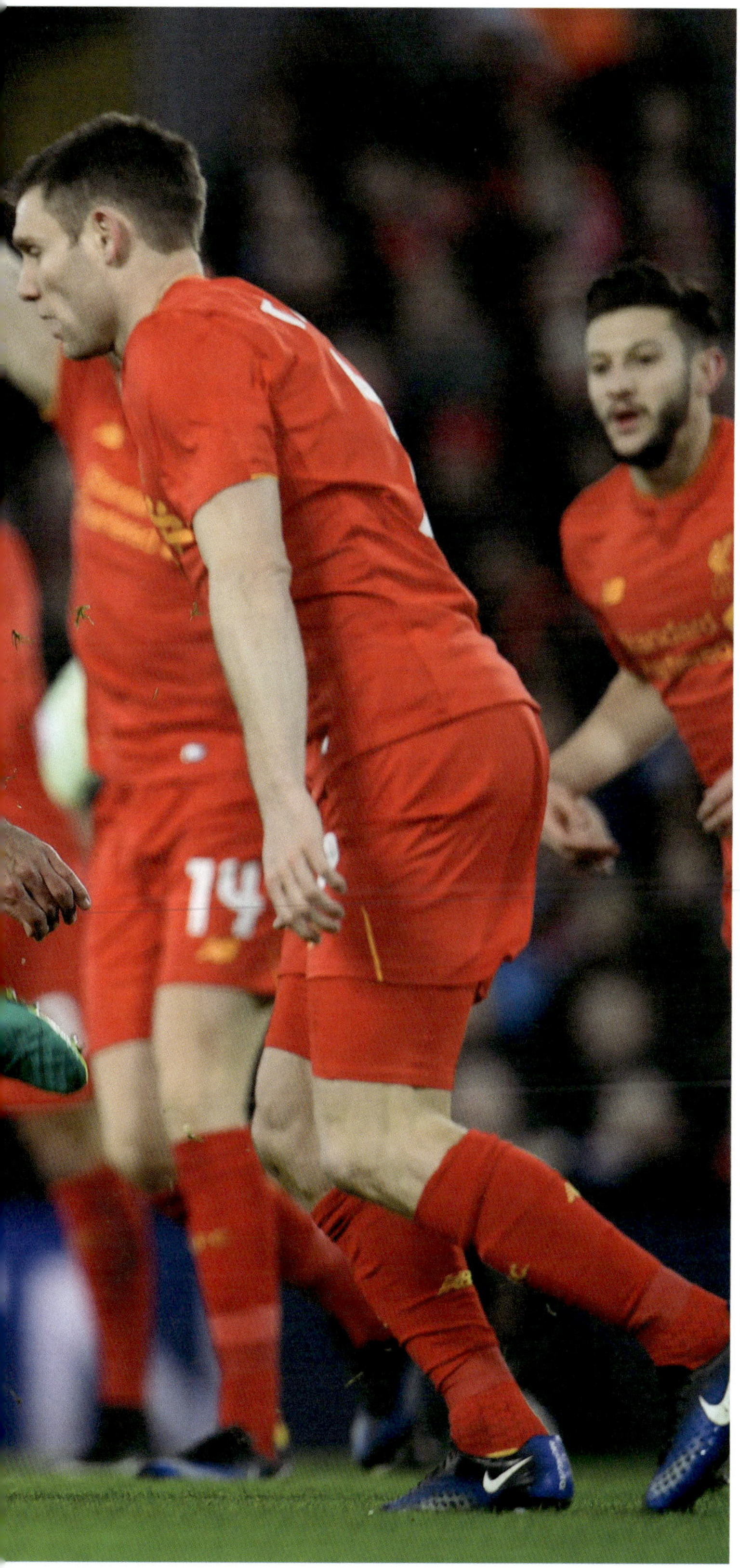

LEFT: Action from the League Cup semi-final at Anfield, where Liverpool entertained Southampton, January 2017.

a manager is like a father figure, and I think that's definitely the case with the manager here. He's really encouraging for young players, it's like he can read your mind. He knows what to say, when to say it and how to say it. There are times he might think you need a bit of a telling off, but there's other times when you might need a bit of encouragement, and that's what he does as well. He knows what to do and when to do it.

"He understands the game unbelievably well, knows what it's like to be a player and knows that mistakes will happen. But he knows it's how you react to them, and how you keep on going, how to play with the team's identity, no matter what the scoreline is, that we have to believe in our ability. The way we want to play is high pressing, win the ball back as high as possible and play football, and that's obviously what we try to do, and he instils that no matter what the score is.

"Without him who knows what would've happened. He's the one that's given me the most opportunities, more than I can even ask for. He's obviously put a lot of trust and faith in me personally and I've tried to repay him every time he's done that. Within his first few weeks, he was down at the Academy watching the young lads. That gave us a bit more faith and gave a statement to the club that he is going to use young players and give us chances."

Back-to-back appearances in the League Cup final however eluded Klopp. Alexander-Arnold started in the 2-0 last eight win against Leeds and the semi-final, second leg against Southampton at Anfield but over the two games against the stubborn Saints, Liverpool could not breach their defences. A first leg 1-0 defeat at St Mary's came only three days after the side had beaten Plymouth in the FA Cup and even though the result, the sixth instalment of a frenetic month of games on three fronts, meant the fatigued Reds had won just once in January there were still high hopes of overturning the deficit in the return match in front of the Kop.

A lacklustre first half did little to rouse the fans but with Anfield echoing to the cries of 'attack, attack, attack' after the break, the home side woke up. Daniel Sturridge had two great chances and Liverpool two strong penalty appeals rejected, the second for handball, but it was not their night on Merseyside and Southampton delivered the knockout blow in second-half injury time with a breakaway goal to wrap up a 2-0 aggregate victory.

"I'm disappointed," Klopp said after the final whistle. "Second half we did much better, created outstanding chances. I don't look for excuses, but it's really hard to accept [bad decisions] week by week by week. The handball was 100 per cent. The performance was OK, we created chances – we didn't score, that's absolutely right. We are a good football playing side, that's why teams [change style to play us]. They won both games, they deserved it. I'm fine with the performance but not the result."

It took Liverpool three further games to return to winning ways – beating Spurs in the Premier League in February – but their New Year troubles were quickly forgotten and in the wake of their Tottenham triumph, the Reds were unbeaten in 11 of their final 12 fixtures. January had been the sternest test of Klopp's managerial reign so far but he had not blinked. "If we would doubt the way we are after this little problems we have now, it would be a strange thing," he said after the second Southampton game. "We know what we have to do."

RIGHT: Klopp lets his feelings known on the touchline at Anfield, where Liverpool faced Middlesbrough in May 2017.

"We know what we have to do."

KYIV CALLING (2017-18)

Restored to the Champions League's fray, Liverpool's European return was box office despite Jürgen Klopp's side ultimately being denied a fairy-tale ending in the final.

The first day of pre-season training was still almost three weeks away when Klopp celebrated the milestone of his 50th birthday in the summer of 2017. Given his unerring obsession with the beautiful game, no doubt his thoughts drifted even during his own party towards the upcoming campaign and the challenges ahead, not least Liverpool's hard-earned return to Champions League duty. Back amongst the continent's fellow heavyweights, the spotlight would shine on the German and his side more brightly than ever before.

Balancing the demands of European football with the Reds' domestic commitments would not be easy. Since Klopp's move to Merseyside, the club's net spend on transfers had been less than £14 million and although there were no public complaints about the strength in depth of his squad, the manager must have privately envied the financial power his team's principal Premier League and European rivals were able to wield in the transfer market. Success can rarely be achieved with money alone but Liverpool certainly needed a blockbuster recruit with the Champions League on the horizon.

ABOVE: The reality of being a Liverpool player sinks in for Mo Salah as he gets his first taste of the Anfield dressing room.

On 1 July, the club announced Mohamed Salah had signed.

On 1 July, the club announced Mohamed Salah had signed. The Egyptian forward joined from Roma for an initial fee of £36.9 million but the deal was structured to potentially rise by £7 million depending on appearances and performance targets. It was a club record for the club and further evidence that Liverpool were, ahead of his third season in the hotseat, prepared to back Klopp for the long term.

There was though a mixed reaction to the news among certain sections of the supporters and the media. Salah hadn't set the world alight during his first spell in England, a two-season stint with Chelsea which yielded just 19 games and two goals, and while he had repaired some of the damage to his reputation in Italy with Roma, the jury was still out on whether Salah was really the player to take Liverpool to the next level.

By the end of his first season on Merseyside there was no doubt. The long list of records Salah broke in 2017-18 read like a scarcely believable storyline from *Roy of the Rovers* and when Klopp unleashed him as the most advanced player in a first-choice

attacking trio alongside Brazilian Roberto Firmino and Sadio Mané, the goals flowed with reassuring regularity. It was no coincidence that the Reds scored an eye-watering 135 times in all competitions during a thrilling campaign.

It would have been easy for Klopp to take all the credit for the transformative impact the Salah signing had on the side but it spoke volumes about his unassuming personality and his belief in the Anfield collective that the German readily acknowledged the

"Our scouting department did a fantastic job around Mo," the manager revealed.

decision to recruit the Egyptian was not his alone.

"Our scouting department did a fantastic job around Mo," the manager revealed. "They just didn't get out of our ears about him. It was '100 per cent he is ready, he is ready'. Of course we had to look at a lot of his games to see about other parts, physicality, being strong enough for challenges. I met him at one point and he looks more sturdy. If you watch him only on TV he looks quite skinny. I didn't make a number [of goals] for him before we signed him. We knew we would get a very offensive-minded midfielder who is a lot of games a striker but also has the ability to make goals, to set up goals. So that was the package we wanted. His speed is his speed, it doesn't depend on which league he's in. That is clear."

The remainder of the transfer window saw the club invest a hefty £40 million to tempt Arsenal to sell England midfielder Alex Oxlade-Chamberlain but the deal that initially went under the radar was the signing of Andy Robertson from Hull City. It cost the club £10 million to land the left-back and although he was already a full Scotland international when the 23-year-old moved to Merseyside, he had only two seasons of Premier League experience with the Tigers. It was a solid but not spectacular CV but Robertson quickly proved to the manor born at Anfield and in tandem with Trent Alexander-Arnold, who had signed a new deal in the summer, began to form arguably the most dynamic full-back pairing in Europe.

VIRGIL'S WATCH BEGINS

A trip to Vicarage Road to face Watford in the league was Liverpool's first assignment of the season. They returned home with a point after a dramatic 3-3 draw after the home side grabbed an injury-time equaliser but encouragingly Salah, Firmino and Mané were all on the scoresheet, an early vindication of Klopp's vision for the team's revamped offensive shape. The Premier League opening fixture was sandwiched by home and away clashes against Hoffenheim in the Champions League play-offs, successfully negotiated with a 6-3 victory on aggregate.

Liverpool were similarly untroubled – and unbeaten – in the group phase of the competition, scoring 26 goals and conceding only six in six outings to progress serenely to the knockout stages in 2018. The team's League Cup campaign started and abruptly ended in September after a 2-0 reverse at Leicester but their league form was unaffected by the early elimination and after they had beaten Burnley 2-1 at Turf Moor on New Year's Day, the Reds were safely established in the top four.

It was events away from the pitch in January however that threatened to derail Liverpool's season. Spanish giants Barcelona had been engaged in a long, persistent and very public pursuit of Brazilian playmaker Philippe Coutinho and the saga came to a head when Liverpool finally accepted an incredible

OPPOSITE: Klopp chats with newcomer Andy Robertson, who proved to be a canny signing for the club.

BELOW: Philippe Coutinho in action for Liverpool, before his departure to Barcelona.

Ten days before Coutinho had left, Liverpool confirmed the signing of Virgil van Dijk from Southampton.

"It is part of life and part of football."

£142 million bid for the star after turning down three earlier offers and a transfer request from the player in the summer.

Losing Coutinho, albeit for such an enormous fee, after his six influential seasons on Merseyside could have been seen as a lack of ambition. Barcelona were after all one of the Reds' main European rivals and, like Klopp's team, through to the Last 16 of the Champions League. Klopp was acutely aware of how the picture could be painted and was front and centre to reassure the fans that Liverpool were not taking a backward step.

"It is totally understandable that supporters will be disappointed," he said. "This is always the case when you have to say goodbye to someone special. But, as hard as it is sometimes to accept, it is part of life and part of football. Individuals have their own dreams and their own goals and objectives in life. Players will come and players will go, that is football, but as a club we are big enough and strong enough to continue with our aggressive progression on the pitch, even when we lose an important player.

"We have never been in a better position in recent times as a club to react in the right way. We will use our size and strength to absorb moments like this and still move forward. I have been here long enough now to know in the history of Liverpool, key players have left before but the club always goes on. You cannot transfer the heart and soul of Liverpool Football Club, although I am sure there are many clubs who would like to buy it."

In truth, Klopp and the club had already done the deal to ensure their 'aggressive progression' would continue. Ten days before Coutinho had left, Liverpool confirmed the signing of Virgil van Dijk from Southampton. The Dutch centre-back cost £75 million, a world record for a defender, but Klopp and the club hierarchy had anticipated the financial windfall on the way from the Coutinho transfer and with the Salah, Mané and Firmino combination looking lethal, the manager decided defensive reinforcements were more important than clinging on to the unsettled Brazilian. It was a brave move but one which paid off handsomely as Van Dijk, almost overnight, showed he was undoubtedly, as Klopp had hoped, the final piece of Liverpool's back-four jigsaw.

OPPOSITE: **Virgil van Dijk settled into his new role at Liverpool with comfortable ease, as Klopp was happy to see.**

CITY DISMISSED, UKRAINE UPSET

The second half of the league campaign eventually brought a repeat of the previous season's fourth place finish. There were only three defeats in the 16-match sequence between January and May, which started most memorably with a pulsating 4-3 victory against Manchester City at Anfield, but Liverpool's place in the top four was not confirmed until the final weekend of fixtures. Losing 1-0 to Chelsea at Stamford Bridge in their penultimate game left Champions League qualification hanging in the balance but the Reds made no mistake at home against Brighton seven days later, running out 4-0 winners to ensure they'd be back in Europe's elite competition next season. This time they would not have to endure the jeopardy of the play-offs with fourth place in the Premier League now guaranteeing automatic progress to the group stages.

Early exits in both domestic cups was an irritation rather than major setback for Klopp and as February dawned, the time had come for the manager to plot a potential path through the European knockout stages.

Liverpool's Last 16 clash with Porto was over after 90 minutes after they thrashed the home side 5-0 at the Estádio do Dragão in the first leg courtesy of a Mané hat-trick. The goalless draw at Anfield that followed was of little note and the Kop faithful waited for the quarter-final draw, made 10 days later, with anticipation. According to Klopp it was no 'big surprise' that his side had reached the last eight for the first time since 2009, while the footballing gods decreed the Reds would renew hostilities with Manchester City.

By the time the two sides met in early April, they had already played home and away in the league. City were the 5-0 victors at the Etihad in September and Liverpool the 4-3 winners at Anfield in January but domestic form and logic would take a back seat in the Champions League. The Reds hit their opponents like a runaway train on Merseyside as Klopp instructed his players to make life as uncomfortable as possible for the visitors. Going forward Liverpool were ruthless and goals from Salah, Oxlade-Chamberlain and Mané in the first 31 minutes secured a thrilling 3-0 win.

OPPOSITE: A delighted Klopp shows his joy after Liverpool had beaten Manchester City in the Champions League quarter-final.

BELOW: Mané celebrates scoring one of his three goals against Porto in the Champions League, February 2018.

"If one team's style is built to destroy City's smooth rhythms and potency, it is Liverpool's high-octane approach under Jürgen Klopp," wrote the BBC's Chief Football Writer Phil McNulty. "And so it proved as all Guardiola's fears were realised. Liverpool were all over City like a rash. As they turned up the pressure, City's flaws, concealed for most of this season, were suddenly exposed. City were rattling

And so it proved as all Guardiola's fears were realised.

and resembled a boxer staggering to his corner as they went off for half-time. As some of City's players shrunk in Anfield's white heat, so many of Liverpool's rose to the occasion."

Unlike in the previous round against Porto however, the second leg was anything but a formality. When City scored at the Etihad after only two minutes, Liverpool supporters braced themselves for a protracted siege on their goal but rather than simply trying to survive, their team opted for attack as the best form of defence and second-half goals from Salah and Firmino gave them a 5-1 triumph over the 180 minutes.

Roma, who had knocked out Barcelona in the previous round, were up next in the semis. A free-flowing 5-2 success in the first leg at Anfield

appeared to have secured a coveted place in the final but before Liverpool headed to the Italian capital, news broke that assistant coach Željko Buvač had left the club. The sudden departure of Klopp's long-term, right-hand man, ending his 17-year association with the German, was far from ideal preparation. The Reds' big night in Rome ultimately proved triumphant, winning 4-2, but their slender 7-6 aggregate win was too close for comfort.

Nonetheless Klopp had taken a side all the way to a Champions League final for the second time in his career. Even for a club with Liverpool's undisputed European pedigree, it was a remarkable achievement given that he had been on Merseyside for less than three years and had inherited a misfiring team suffering a crisis of confidence and identity. Whatever the manager's schedule for his Anfield project, he could not have truly thought the biggest game in European club football would have come quite so soon.

Staged at the Olympic Stadium in Kyiv, the final against Real Madrid was a match between two of the competitions biggest historical hitters. The Spaniards had won the previous two finals while Liverpool were in search of their first crown since 2005 but with the self-belief instilled by Klopp into his players, the Reds were undoubtedly capable of lifting the famous trophy for a sixth time. Their collective conviction however suffered a body blow in the 26th minute in the Ukrainian capital when Salah was sent crashing down following what was at best a clumsy challenge from Madrid captain Sergio Ramos. The impact of the fall dislocated Salah's shoulder and although the Egyptian bravely tried to continue and ignore the pain, the damage had been done and Klopp was

ABOVE: **Jürgen Klopp faces the media in Kyiv, Ukraine.**

OPPOSITE: **Mané is joyous after scoring for Liverpool in the Champions League final against Real Madrid.**

Staged at the Olympic Stadium in Kyiv, the final against Real Madrid was a match between two of the competitions biggest historical hitters.

"We started well and played exactly like we wanted to."

forced to substitute his distraught star winger.

Despite the devastating loss of Salah's goal threat, Liverpool showed their now trademark steely resolve despite a second heartbreaking moment in the 51st minute. Goalkeeper Loris Karius collected a speculative pass in his area safely enough but then inexplicably gave Karim Benzema the chance to block his ill-judged underarm throw out and score a soft, deflating goal with the deflection. The Reds bounced back when Mané equalised only four minutes later but an unbelievable bicycle kick from Gareth Bale restored Real's lead before the Welshman scored a second from long range for which Karius was again at fault, failing to stop a shot directed straight at him which slipped through his fingers.

"The plan is only to play to win, nothing else, [there is] not a lot to say," admitted Klopp after the agonising loss. "We started well and played exactly like we wanted to. The situation with Sergio Ramos [and Mohamed Salah] looked really bad and it was a shock for the team, we lost the positive momentum and they immediately came up. What can I say about the goals? We scored one, they scored three."

Defeat was of course a bitter pill to swallow. The Salah substitution and errors in goal had not been part of Klopp's plan and in a contest that was otherwise evenly balanced, the game could easily have swung the other way. The Liverpool dressing

room may have been an understandably unhappy one after the final whistle but many were able to put the long campaign in a far more positive context.

"Klopp has been a transformative personality," wrote Barney Ronay in *The Guardian*. "He is wonderfully charming. He has done a wonderful, alchemical job with this group of players. The Liverpool manager has worked wonders this season but his high-octane squad now needs some investment from the board to compete on the biggest stage. He has provided a wonderful service to Liverpool's owners, forcing the club back to the grand stage of European football, opening up lusty revenue streams and at no point questioning the resources at his disposal.

ABOVE: Salah in control of the ball before his shoulder injury and fateful substitution.

OPPOSITE: Roberto Firmino clashes spectacularly for the ball with Sergio Ramos of Real Madrid.

"Liverpool FC is in rude health thanks to the successful ground redevelopment, and above all the good vibes, the basic positivity created by the spectacle of full-speed Klopp-ball. There is another side to this: Klopp is a stayer. Fight, run, harry and be damned has been a wonderful Plan A this season. Liverpool can bask in the memories of some genuinely thrilling, high-spec football. But as ever with Klopp this is a moment not to stop, but instead to press even harder."

"Liverpool FC is in rude health thanks to the successful ground redevelopment, and above all the good vibes, the basic positivity created by the spectacle of full-speed Klopp-ball."

The record-breaking form of Salah was, of course, an enormous cause for optimism as the Reds licked their wounds in Kyiv. His shoulder would heal in time for the new season and although he did not score in the final before his premature exit, what he had achieved in his debut year for the club was breathtaking. Astutely deployed by Klopp in an advanced position on the right of the team's attacking trio, giving him licence to cut inside and create havoc with his lethal left foot, the Egyptian was unplayable.

His total of 44 goals in just 49 appearances in all competitions was the highest individual haul for the club since Ian Rush had scored 47 back in 1983-84. His goal against Brighton in May took him to 32 in the league, earning him the coveted Golden Boot award and breaking the record for a 38-game Premier League season previously held jointly at 31 by Alan Shearer, Luis Suárez and Cristiano Ronaldo. His scoring exploits in his first campaign eclipsed the milestones of both Robbie Fowler and Fernando Torres for the best return in a debut year. Salah also netted 11 times in Europe, making the first ever Liverpool player to reach double figures in a single Champions League season. From Roger Hunt and Rush to Kenny Dalglish and Fowler, the Reds had always been blessed with some of the game's greatest goalscorers and in Salah they now had another to rank amongst them.

ECSTASY AND AGONY (2018-19)

The goalkeeping heroics came in the side's Champions League clash with Napoli in December.

BELOW: Alisson Becker saves outstandingly for Liverpool against Arkadiusz Milik of Napoli.

European champions for a sixth time and record-breaking runners-up in the Premier League, it was a rollercoaster season on Merseyside which climaxed with Jürgen Klopp's first silverware at Anfield.

Football is a game frequently decided by the finest of margins. The difference between elite teams is often only marginal and as Klopp prepared for his third full season as Liverpool manager he could not have envisaged that the upcoming campaign would be ultimately be defined by two seminal moments which both had a dramatic impact on the club's fortunes. One was a single, world-class save which almost lifted the roof off Anfield, the other an implausible goal-line clearance that denied the Reds a place in the history books.

The goalkeeping heroics came in the side's Champions League clash with Napoli in December. Having already lost their three away games in the group stages to the Italians, Paris Saint-Germain and Red Star Belgrade, Liverpool needed to win with a clean sheet or by two clear goals to save their faltering European challenge and progress to the Last 16. Mohamed Salah's goal in the 34th minute gave Klopp's side hope but second-half injury time on Merseyside threatened disaster when Napoli

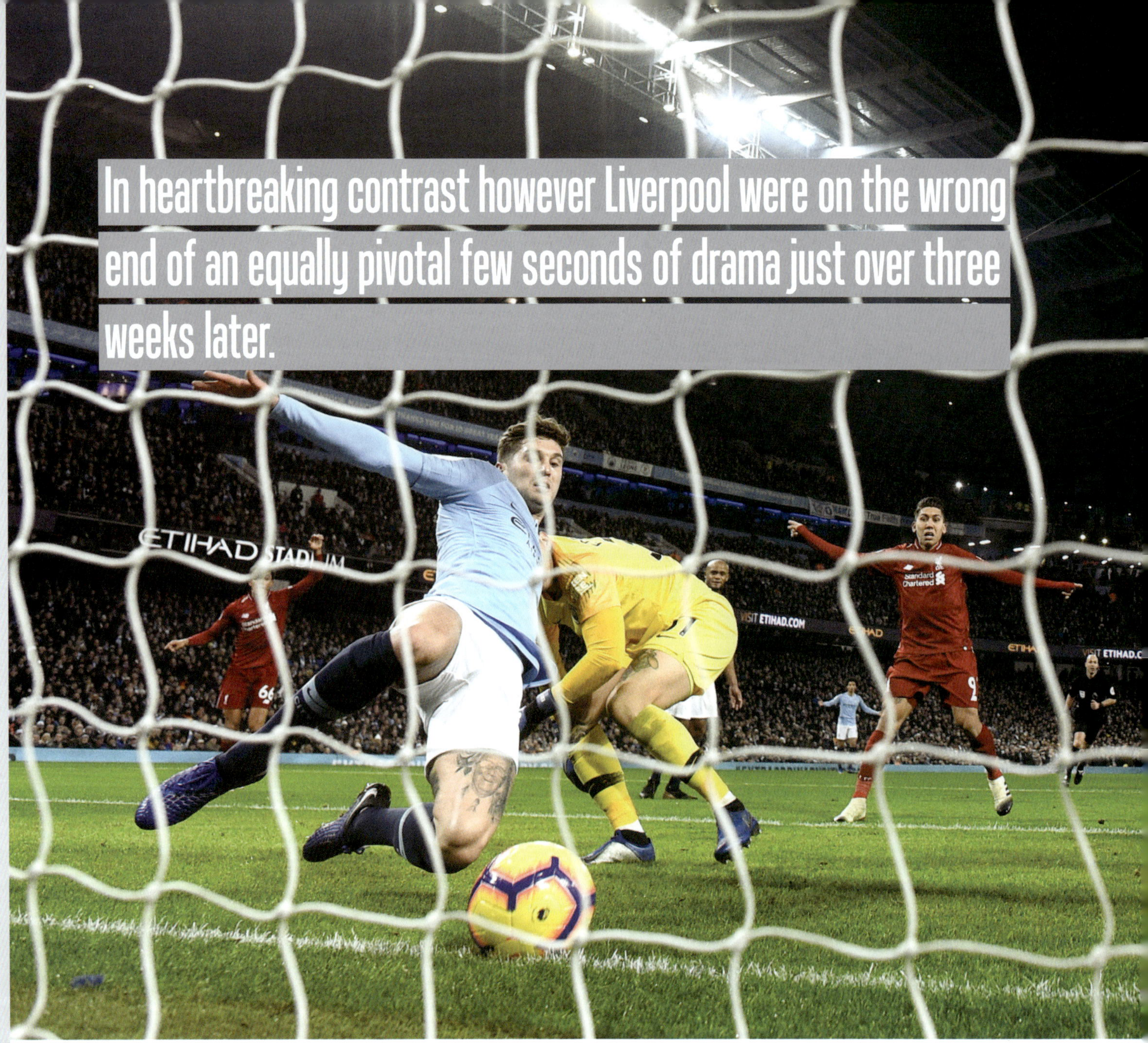

In heartbreaking contrast however Liverpool were on the wrong end of an equally pivotal few seconds of drama just over three weeks later.

striker Arkadiusz Milik found space just six yards out. He had to score from point blank range but keeper Alisson spread himself and somehow saved with his right thigh. Liverpool survived and courtesy of that split second moment of brilliance were handed the reprieve that paved the way for the team to lift the Champions League trophy six months later.

"If I knew Alisson was this good, I would have paid double," a breathless Klopp said at full-time, referencing the £66.8 million the club paid for the player in the summer, a world record for a goalkeeper. "I have no words for that. That was the lifesaver tonight. It was wild and there were lots of counter attacks but we were ready for that. That is Anfield live and in colour. Wow, what a game. I am not sure a manager could be prouder of a team than I am."

In heartbreaking contrast however Liverpool were on the wrong end of an equally pivotal few seconds of drama just over three weeks later. Unbeaten in their opening 20 Premier League games and top of

LEFT: An outstretched John Stones of Manchester City saves the day for his team, denying the predatory instincts of Liverpool's Mo Salah.

the table, the Reds were mounting their strongest title challenge yet under Klopp when they travelled to the Etihad to face Manchester City in early January. The match was, tantalisingly, goalless when City defender John Stones blasted a clearance against his own goalkeeper, the ball bounced back towards goal and Salah, lurking in the six-yard box, seemed certain to score from the rebound only for Stones to stretch out his right leg and remarkably hook the ball off the line. City went on to win the game 2-1 while the technology later revealed that the ball had failed to completely cross the line by just 1.12 cm.

If Liverpool had folded in the second half of the domestic season following the disappointment of that defeat, it would be reasonable to argue that Stones's incredible intervention had not been the one decisive factor in the battle for the Premier League trophy. In fact, the Reds did not lose again in their final 17 league fixtures, winning 13, but it was still not enough to stop City being crowned champions by a single point. Klopp's team had been denied the title and a historic unbeaten season. No one can ever know if Liverpool would have taken priceless points at the Etihad had it not been for Stones's telescopic leg but Klopp would not be human if he had not played the moment over in his head in the years since.

STATEMENT SUMMER SIGNINGS

One of Klopp's greatest achievements in his first two summer transfer windows had been his ability to renew and refresh his squad with a modest net spend. There had been sizeable individual deals running into eight figures, most notably the Salah signing, but given the transfer fees received by the club over the same period, the manager had more than balanced the books and not enjoyed the same financial muscle available to his principal rivals in order to compete.

By the summer of 2018 however the Liverpool ownership realised the time had come to rectify the situation and try to match the deep pockets of the two Manchester clubs and Chelsea in particular. The record-breaking deal to bring Alisson from Roma was a clear statement of intent and the Reds also spent big on midfielders Naby Keita from RB Leipzig, as well as Fabinho from Monaco, and also signed Swiss playmaker Xherdan Shaqiri from Stoke City. The club had committed millions in the window on the quartet of new recruits and with Emre Can the only notable player to bid farewell to Merseyside over the summer, Liverpool had decisively strengthened their hand.

"Jürgen Klopp has spent big to address the weaknesses exposed in the Champions League final and the squad looks well equipped to challenge Manchester City for the title," wrote Andy Hunter in *The Guardian*. "Having invested over £170m in

"Jürgen Klopp has spent big to address the weaknesses exposed in the Champions League final and the squad looks well equipped to challenge Manchester City for the title."

a squad that reached the Champions League final three months ago, Klopp cannot and does not shy from an expectation he has created. More points, more outstanding performances and an improvement on last season's fourth-placed finish would all represent evidence of sustained progress, he has explained. A formidable obstacle stands in the way of Liverpool and that elusive 19th league championship. It is the team they have beaten three times in competitive fixtures this calendar year. It is testament to Klopp's rebuilding work since October 2015, last season's exhilarating run to the Champions League final and a productive summer in the transfer market that his squad appear supremely well-equipped to honour their side of the deal."

New players aside, Klopp had to address the vacancy created in his coaching set-up by the sudden departure of the hugely influential Željko Buvač in April. The manager decided continuity was the best policy and turned to 37-year-old Dutchman Pep Lijnders to become his assistant alongside Peter Krawietz. A former Liverpool Under-16s coach and then first team development coach, Lijnders returned to Anfield after a brief spell with NEC Nijmegen in his native Holland and with his appointment and the summer transfer business both completed, Klopp was as prepared as possible for the ups and downs of the season ahead.

A taste of things to come was served up on the opening day of the Premier League as West Ham were put to the sword at Anfield and sent home on the back of a 4-0 defeat. It was not until late September that the Reds dropped points for the first time after Chelsea, who were also unbeaten, held Klopp's side 1-1 at Stamford Bridge. An eye-catching

89th-minute score from Daniel Sturridge was required to earn the visitors a share of the spoils in London while it was honours even again a week later as both defences dominated when Liverpool hosted City on Merseyside and ended in a collector's item of a goalless draw. After the final whistle Klopp and his opposite number Pep Guardiola both expressed satisfaction at the result, demonstrating the mutual respect between the title-chasing two sides.

Liverpool's march continued from October through to December. The sequence included a rousing 3-1 victory over Manchester United at Anfield before Christmas, Shaqiri coming off the bench to score twice and become only the second Liverpool player ever to register a double against the Mancunians on debut in the fixture. At the end of the same month, the side destroyed Arsenal 5-1 at Anfield courtesy of a Roberto Firmino hat-trick to extend the Reds' lead at the top of the table over second-place Tottenham to nine points.

Liverpool's march continued from October through to December.

BELOW: **Xherdan Shaqiri scores the second goal for Liverpool in their win over Manchester United in December, 2018.**

And then came the New Year and the return game against City in Manchester. After Stones's desperate clearance, Sergio Agüero gave the home side the lead in the 40th minute with a near-post drive only for Firmino to level midway into the second half with a low header. German Leroy Sané made it 2-1 to City 18 minutes from time and although both teams could have scored in a frenetic finale, the Reds could not overturn the deficit.

"Liverpool's disappointment was clear as manager Jürgen Klopp and his players trudged off at the end of their first league defeat of the season, a result that backed up Klopp's insistence that this title race has a long way to run," *BBC Sport* reported from the Etihad. "The Reds were not at their intense best, although they can look back at Mané hitting the post and several other scrambles as key moments that went against them.

"They will be disappointed at the manner of City's opener as Agüero, with a brilliant finish, preyed on the fatal hesitation of Lovren, who had a thoroughly forgettable night. Yet once the frustration subsides, Liverpool can reflect on a superb start to the season that has left them with clear daylight at the summit, something that looked so unlikely just a few weeks ago. They are still in the position everyone wants to occupy."

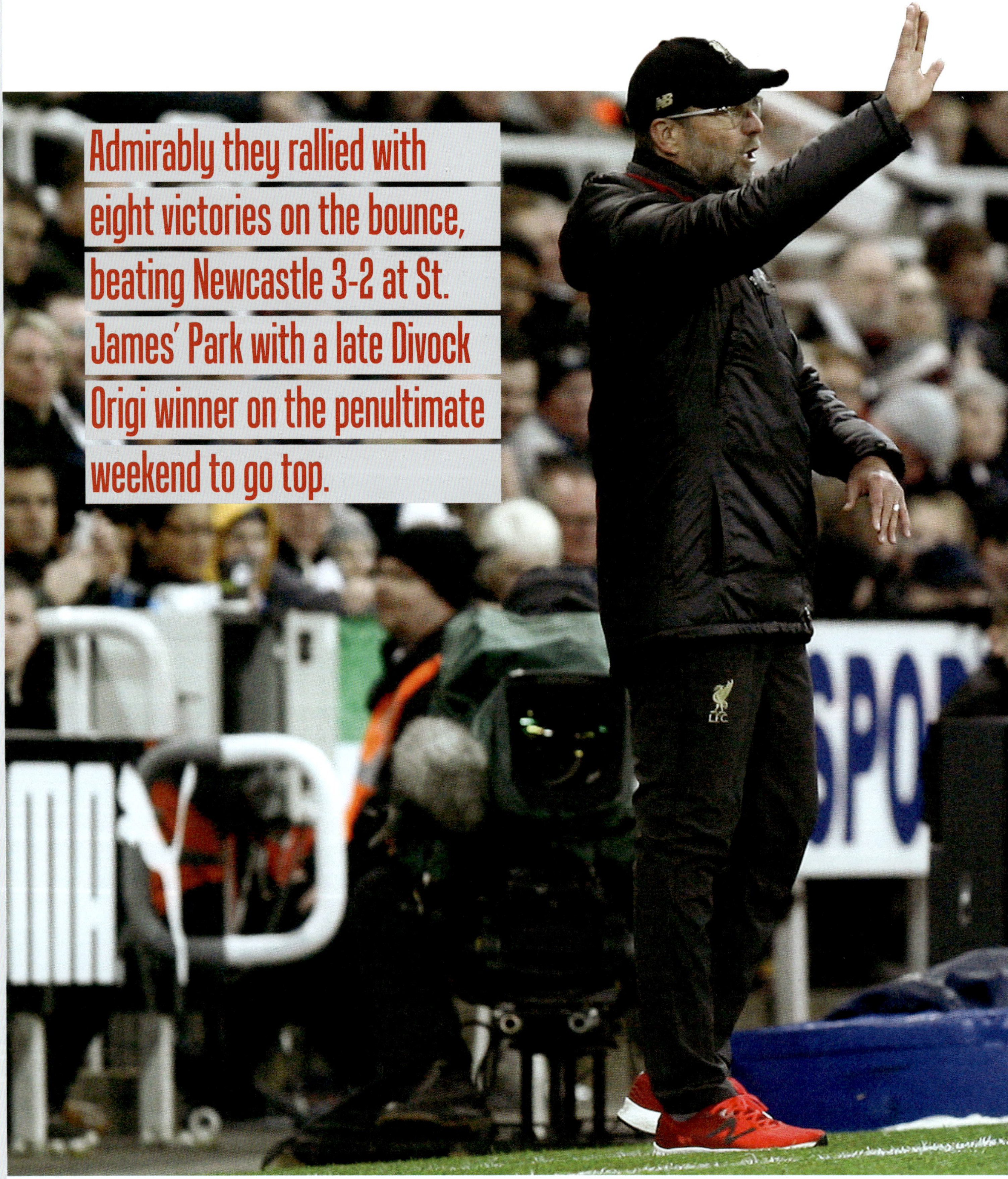

Admirably they rallied with eight victories on the bounce, beating Newcastle 3-2 at St. James' Park with a late Divock Origi winner on the penultimate weekend to go top.

It was a cruel climax to a superb domestic season.

OPPOSITE: Klopp dishes out instructions from the touchline at the St. James' Park Newcastle game, where Liverpool were victorious.

There was little more Klopp and his players could have done to remain on that summit. They immediately bounced from the loss to City with a hard-fought 1-0 win at Brighton thanks to a Salah penalty but their form in February and early March was crucially not quite as imperious as before and although unbeaten, they dropped points following draws against Leicester, West Ham, Man United and in the derby against Everton at Goodison.

Admirably they rallied with eight victories on the bounce, beating Newcastle 3-2 at St. James' Park with a late Divock Origi winner on the penultimate weekend to go top but, two days later, City recaptured pole position after narrowly beating Leicester. It was going down to the wire and although Liverpool did their job in beating Wolves 2-0, they had to hope City would fall at their final hurdle on the road against Brighton. The Citizens did not oblige though, winning 4-1 on the south coast and, adrift by only solitary point, Klopp's team were reluctantly saddled with the unwanted tag of English football's greatest (and unluckiest) top-flight runners-up.

It was a cruel climax to a superb domestic season. Unbeaten at Anfield in 19 league outings, Liverpool had the meanest defence in the division, conceding just 22 times, and the second most prolific attack with 89 goals. Salah and Mané's 22 Premier League strikes apiece saw the Reds pair share the Golden Boot award with Arsenal's Pierre-Emerick Aubameyang. The club's wait for the title however, now 29 painful years, was still not over but despite their frustration, the supporters were in no doubt what Klopp and his players had achieved.

"It seems almost surreal that a team can lose a single game in the world's toughest league yet still come up short," wrote Alex Malone on the This Is Anfield website. "Ninety-seven points would have won England's top division in 116 of the 119 seasons it has been in existence, 2.55 points per game is by far and away Liverpool's best ever points per game total in our illustrious 127-year history, eclipsing the 2.33 points per game in the 1978-79 season.

"I still occasionally pinch myself to make sure we really do have Jürgen Klopp as our manager. No one else in world football could possibly be such a perfect match for our glorious club, our unique culture, our magnificent city and our unrivalled history.

"This is a man so fiercely dedicated in his role as custodian of our club, yet so humble and gracious in his approach. Klopp's approach is that there is no bigger club than Liverpool Football Club. He saw absolutely no reason why English football's most successful club should bow down to anyone. He saw a club with over 600 million fans worldwide (and growing) going about their business saddled with an unwarranted inferiority complex. And he told us, right up front.

"He reprimanded us for leaving the ground early. He scolded us for being doubters. He reminded us that holding your head low is for others but holding your head up high is quintessential Liverpool. He woke us up as fans, and as a club. We were, to use a well-worn but accurate phrase, 'a sleeping giant', but until the arrival of Klopp there were few signs the slumber was over. In little over three and a half years, he has transformed just about everything. The entire club is mirroring the manager. It is smiling again, it is positive again, it is defiant again and we all believe again."

REDEMPTION IN MADRID

To suggest Klopp had unfinished business in the Champions League after the misery of defeat to Real Madrid in June was an understatement. Reaching the final may have been ahead of schedule but that meant little to the manager and his players as they trudged off the pitch in Ukraine while their opposite

To suggest Klopp had unfinished business in the Champions League after the misery of defeat to Real Madrid in June was an understatement.

numbers celebrated wildly. Adversity however can be harnessed to whet the appetite rather than diminish confidence and the Reds were determined to lay the ghosts of Kyiv to rest.

Their bid to do that began in September with the kind of drama that would be a feature of their European adventure. French heavyweights PSG were the visitors to Anfield and the Reds appeared to be cruising to a comfortable victory after first-half goals from Sturridge and then Milner from the spot. PSG hit back with two scores and in second-half injury time it was level at 2-2 before substitute Firmino claimed the three points with an angled low drive. Liverpool's poor away form in the group stage almost derailed their challenge and Anfield was heavily indebted to Allison's heroics against Napoli to ensure their side did not falter at the first hurdle. The Reds narrowly went through as runners-up behind PSG but only because they had scored more goals (nine to seven) than the Italians, who also accumulated nine points in their six games.

Despite a goalless stalemate on Merseyside in the first leg of their Last 16 clash against Bayern Munich, Liverpool despatched the reigning Bundesliga champions in the return fixture in Germany with surprising ease. A brace from Mané and a third from Virgil van Dijk ensured Joel Matip's own goal was no more than a footnote in the match, which ended

3-1. It was also relatively anxiety free in the last eight as the Reds wrapped up a 6-1 aggregate success against Porto as Firmino scored home and away.

Facing Barcelona in the semi-finals was though an altogether different and, even for Liverpool, more daunting prospect.

Facing Barcelona in the semi-finals was though an altogether different and, even for Liverpool, more daunting prospect. The Spanish had claimed yet another La Liga title the previous season and with Lionel Messi in their ranks, the Catalans were as ever a force to be reckoned with. The Reds may not

ABOVE: **Georginio Wijnaldum scores a thumping header in the Champions League semi-final against Barcelona.**

have feared Barcelona but they were acutely aware they represented their most serious challenge yet. The first leg at the Nou Camp at the start of May only reinforced that as the home side cut loose and two goals from Messi – the second his 600th for the club – and former Red Luis Suárez gave Barcelona a seemingly decisive 3-0 triumph.

The media devoted thousands of column inches to the hopelessness of Liverpool's task at Anfield in the return leg six short days later. Klopp of course was unmoved by the negativity and repeatedly insisted his side were not ready to wave the white flag. "There's hope and it's football," he said. "If we can do it, wonderful. If we can't do it, let's fail in the most beautiful way." His relentless optimism however must surely have wavered when his medical staff told the manager that Salah, Firmino and Naby Keita were injured and unavailable.

What unfolded in the second leg on Merseyside was nothing short of a football fairy tale. Liverpool desperately needed an early goal to stoke the fires of both the players and the crowd and they got it after seven minutes when Origi tapped in from close range but it was not until midway through the second-half that Anfield began to truly believe. The lifeline came in the space of just 122 seconds as midfielder Georginio Wijnaldum twice appeared in the box to convert crosses from Trent Alexander-

ABOVE: Nerves jangling, Klopp in training on the eve of the Champions League final against Tottenham Hotspur.

RIGHT: Overhead shot of a jubilant Salah after scoring from a spot kick in the opening few seconds of the game.

Klopp had reached the third Champions League final of his career.

Arnold and then Shaqiri and suddenly level the tie at 3-3. The decibel levels inside Anfield were now off the scale and the world famous old stadium shook to its foundations 11 minutes from time when Origi benefitted from Alexander-Arnold's quick-thinking from a corner and turned in the winner with a curling, first-time effort. One of the greatest ever escapes in football was complete.

"Liverpool are into their second successive Champions League final after overcoming Barcelona with a stunning second-leg fightback on an epic night at Anfield" said the *BBC Sport* website. "Roared on relentlessly by their fans, the Reds produced an incredible all-action display to claw back and then ultimately overturn their 3-0 deficit from the Nou Camp with an unanswered four-goal salvo in thrilling style. It is the first time since 1986 – when Barcelona knocked out Gothenburg in the old European Cup – that a team have recovered a three-goal first-leg deficit to win a semi-final in this competition.

"Anfield was rocking and the home fans stayed on their feet to cheer their side home in the closing minutes, with a shell-shocked Barça side unable to fashion any serious response. The final whistle brought delirious celebrations on the pitch and in the stands, where the Reds supporters had played their part in an unforgettable match. Liverpool have managed famous European fightbacks before, notably when they won this competition for the fifth time in Istanbul in 2005, but this was arguably the greatest in their glittering history."

It was Salah who stepped forward to take the penalty.

ABOVE: Steven Gerrard and Rafa Benitez proudly display the Champions League trophy in 2005 – Liverpool's last win.

Klopp had reached the third Champions League final of his career. For only the second time in the history of the competition it would be an all-English affair with Liverpool facing Tottenham at the Metropolitano Stadium in Madrid. A sixth European crown was the prize on offer for the Reds and for Klopp the enticing opportunity to join Bob Paisley, Joe Fagan and Rafael Benitez as European Cup winning managers with the Reds. Even the late, great Bill Shankly had not lifted the famous trophy during his record-breaking Anfield reign.

Both Salah and Firmino were restored to Klopp's starting XI for the match and it was the Egyptian who made an immediate impact in Spain. Mané received the ball in the Spurs box but his cross hit the arm of midfielder Moussa Sissoko only 21 seconds after kick-off and the referee dramatically pointed to the spot. It was Salah who stepped forward to take the penalty, going to the left of goalkeeper Hugo Lloris with a powerful, rising effort. With just one minute and 48 seconds on the clock when the ball slammed into the back of the net, it was the second fastest goal in the history of Champions League finals.

If Klopp hoped the quick-fire score might signal a comfortable canter to the trophy, he was disappointed. After the break, Spurs intensified the pressure and were it not for Alisson in goal, the Londoners could have levelled. The Reds needed another goal to settle the contest and the nerves were finally transformed to joy in the 87th minute by Origi. A corner which they failed to clear created panic in the Tottenham area and the Belgian striker was on hand to unleash a superb low drive into the far bottom corner. There was no time for any further twists and as the referee blew the final whistle, Liverpool had returned to the pinnacle of European club football once again.

"Without this manager this is impossible," Reds captain Jordan Henderson said in Madrid. "You go

"Without this manager this is impossible," Reds captain Jordan Henderson said in Madrid.

through tough times in a season, but what he has done since coming in is unbelievable. There's such a togetherness, he has created a special dressing room. All the praise goes to the manager." After the game, the German himself was clearly emotional and insisted his side's famous victory was the fruits of collective sacrifice. "I am so happy for the boys all these people, and my family," he said. "They suffer

BELOW: Divock Origi scores Liverpool's second goal among the stricken Spurs defence.

The nerves were finally transformed to joy in the 87th minute by Origi.

ABOVE: Jordan Henderson along with the whole team show their ecstasy on lifting the European crown once again.

RIGHT: Klopp sucks up the cheers and adulation from an emotional Liverpool crowd parade.

for me, they deserve it more than anybody. It is the best night of our professional lives. It was an intense season with the most beautiful finish I ever could have imagined."

MATCH STATS

CHAMPIONS LEAGUE FINAL 2019

Saturday, 1 June 2019
(Metropolitano Stadium, Madrid; attendance 63,272)

Liverpool (1) 2 – Tottenham Hotspur (0) 0
(Salah 2 (pen), Origi 87)

Liverpool: Alisson; Alexander-Arnold, Matip, Van Dijk, Robertson, Henderson, Fabinho, Wijnaldum (Milner 62), Salah, Firmino (Origi 58), Mané (Gomez 90).

THE TITLE COMES HOME (2019-20)

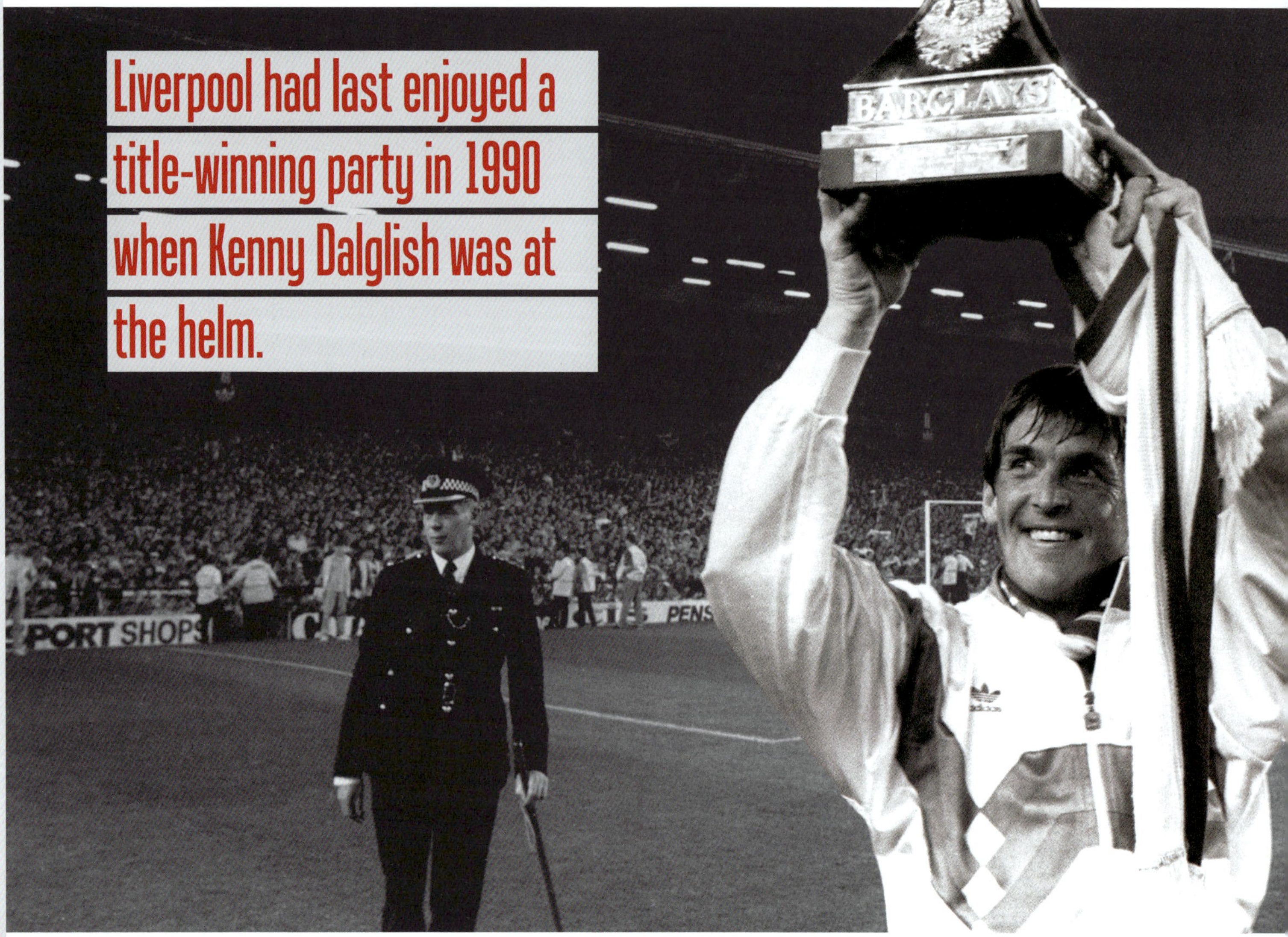

Liverpool had last enjoyed a title-winning party in 1990 when Kenny Dalglish was at the helm.

After 30 years of hurt, Jürgen Klopp became a true Liverpool legend after delivering the prize of the Premier League in a campaign that proved to be like no other before.

If you had canvassed the Anfield faithful, before the beginning of 2018-19, whether they could choose to be crowned the champions of England or Europe, it's debatable what their response would have been. After nine full-throttle months of football, the team came gloriously close to lifting both trophies but with the highest-profile piece of continental silverware secured after their triumph over Tottenham in the Champions League final, there was no doubt what the fans yearned for in the summer of 2019. Liverpool had last enjoyed a title-winning party in 1990 when Kenny Dalglish was at the helm and after three frustrating decades waiting unexpectedly for a repeat performance, the supporters' prolonged patience was almost exhausted.

Since Dalglish's hugely successful first six-year reign – the legendary Scot won three top-flight titles – six successive permanent managers had come and gone at Anfield with varying degrees of success but all failed to deliver the Holy Grail of a 19th Championship for the club. Under the contrasting reigns of Graeme Souness, Roy Evans, Gérard Houllier, Rafa Benítez, Roy Hodgson and Brendan Rodgers between 1991 and 2015, the club never finished lower than eighth in the table but while it was a record of consistency many other clubs would envy, Liverpool's ambitions were loftier and unfulfilled.

OPPOSITE: 'King' Kenny Dalglish with the First Division trophy in 1990. Little did Liverpool know at the time, that the next would be an incredible 30 years later.

Dalglish himself even returned for a second stint in the dugout in 2011, resuming control for 74 games, but in whatever managerial direction the club turned, the result was disappointingly the same. Before Klopp swept into Merseyside in 2015, there had been four near misses in the shape of second-place finishes in the barren years but none of the coaches who were tasked with following in Dalglish's legendary footsteps before or after his second spell were able to take the team over the elusive winning line.

All of the campaigns that followed the 1990 triumph of course began with hope and belief. Every season the Reds were tipped as challengers but every year they were eventually the bridesmaids and not the bride. The mood looking expectantly towards 2019-20 however was genuinely different. Liverpool had already proved in 2018-19 they had the talent, the stamina, the attacking threat, the defensive resolve and the right manager to challenge over 38 games and as the Anfield faithful reflected on what might have been, the conclusion was the chances of a side losing just one league game all season and still not becoming champions was a heartbreaking anomaly that would probably never be repeated. As Klopp himself said philosophically, "it was not far away from a perfect season, but it was not perfect."

ADRIÁN SPOT ON

His side's exhilarating trophy assault on two fronts in 2018-19 convinced Klopp that his squad was well equipped to go again the following season and so it was an unremarkable summer transfer window in

The Premier League then took a temporary back seat as Liverpool flew out to Turkey for the UEFA Super Cup.

terms of new signings. A number of the Reds' older guard, including Daniel Sturridge, Danny Ings, Alberto Moreno and Simon Mignolet, did leave Anfield but in large part the manager decided to put his faith in the same group of players for his fifth campaign in charge. Domestic duties began in early August with their Premier League opener at home against newly promoted Norwich City. An own goal after seven minutes was the worst possible start for the visitors and the Reds were not in charitable mood, scoring further goals through Mohamed Salah, Virgil van Dijk and Divock Origi to register a 4-1 victory and kick off their season in style.

The Premier League then took a temporary back seat as Liverpool flew out to Turkey for the UEFA Super Cup, the annual one-off clash between the previous season's Champions and Europa League winners, who in 2019 were Chelsea. Istanbul was their destination,

LEFT: Hero keeper Adrián awaits celebrations from the team as his dramatic penalty save secured the Reds victory in the UEFA Super Cup in Istanbul, Turkey.

the same city if not the same stadium – this time it was the Beşiktaş Stadium rather than the Ataturk Olympic Stadium – where the Reds had famously come back from three goals down against AC Milan to lift the European Cup 14 years earlier. Even before kick-off, it was match of milestones with a first ever all-English showdown in the fixture, French referee Stéphanie Frappart becoming the first woman to take charge of a major European men's game and, ahead of the upcoming Champions League that season, the debut deployment of VAR in the Super Cup.

Liverpool's hopes of lifting the trophy for a fourth time following wins in 1977, 2001 and 2005 were jolted when Chelsea took the lead three minutes into the second half. Sadio Mané levelled proceedings to take the match into extra-time on a swelteringly hot night in Turkey and when the Senegalese forward scored a second, the Reds were on course to avoid the madness of a shootout. A Chelsea penalty however put paid to that plan and the match had to be decided from the spot.

Step forward goalkeeper Adrián. Just nine days before the fixture, the Spanish stopper had been without a club after he was released by West Ham at the end of the previous season and on the same day

Step forward goalkeeper Adrián. Just nine days before the fixture, the Spanish stopper had been without a club after he was released by West Ham.

that Mignolet moved to Belgium and Club Brugge, Klopp made his move and Adrián joined the club on a free transfer. The 32-year-old was signed as cover for Alisson but was pressed into first team action far earlier than expected when the Brazilian suffered a calf injury in the Norwich game and Adrián was summoned from the bench at Anfield. Alisson failed to recover in time for the trip to Istanbul and the new goalkeeper unexpectedly started for the club for the first time in Turkey.

The shootout saw both teams convert their first four penalties apiece. Salah was on target with the

"It was all about winning it and we did that in the end."

fifth for the Reds to make it 5-4 and when Adrián strolled back into the area to face Tammy Abraham's effort, he knew a successful save would hand the team the trophy. Abraham went to the left but Adrián gambled on going to the opposite side of the goal, diving to the right. But all was not lost and when he realised he had guessed wrong, he instinctively stuck out his right leg to make the stop. He had little time to dwell on his heroics as he was mobbed by the team-mates who he had only met for the first time less than a fortnight ago.

"It was a very difficult game for both teams," a proud Klopp admitted after clinching the second major honour of his Anfield tenure. "It was all about winning it and we did that in the end. Nobody in the stadium wanted extra time, it was a killer. I'm not sure about the penalty but who cares now. We started well then dropped off. We could talk about football but it's too late now. We had to fight and the boys did tonight." The manager was also understandably full of praise for his new goalkeeper in what was only his second appearance for the club. "What a story! Adrián! Like Rocky, after he lost against Apollo Creed. A great, wonderful story. He kept his nerves together. He's really loud in the dressing room already. He's Spanish, the emotions come through. It's all good. It's so nice for him. I don't think he's won a lot in his life so it's so nice to win this really big one and be an

MATCH STATS

UEFA SUPER CUP 2019

Wednesday, 14 August 2019
(Vodafone Park, Istanbul; attendance 38,434)

Liverpool (0) 2 – Chelsea (1) 2 (aet)
(Mané 48, 95) – (Giroud 36, Jorginho 101 (pen))

Liverpool: Adrián; Gomez, Matip, Van Dijk, Robertson (Alexander-Arnold 90), Henderson, Fabinho, Milner (Wijnaldum 64), Salah, Mané (Origi 103), Oxlade-Chamberlain (Firmino 46).

important part in that game as well."

Resting on their laurels after winning in Istanbul was not an option. Just three days later the side were on the South Coast to play Southampton at St Mary's but showed no signs of a hangover, literal or metaphoric, from their energy-sapping exertions in Istanbul. Mané and Roberto Firmino were both on target and although Adrián slammed his late attempted clearance against the shins of Ings to gift the erstwhile Red a goal, Liverpool wrapped up a 2-1 win. The result equalled the club's record of 11 Premier League wins in succession, which had begun with their 4-2 victory over Burnley at Anfield the previous season back in March.

Eleven back-to-back successes became 12 in late August when Klopp masterminded a 3-1 defeat of Arsenal on Merseyside. Their dozen three-point hauls in a row set a new record for the club in the Premier League era and also equalled the 12 consecutive top-flight league wins Kenny Dalglish's side posted in 1990. Klopp's team, albeit only three games into

ABOVE: **Jürgen takes centre glory to celebrate winning the UEFA Super Cup, with his coaching staff.**

OPPOSITE: **Klopp offering his wisdom from the touchline.**

the new campaign, were flying and top of the table. It was a lofty position the Reds refused to relinquish for the rest of a season that proved to be unique in more ways than one.

REDS RULE THE WORLD

Following the Gunners game, the wins just kept coming as Liverpool's season gathered pace. By the end of September Klopp had already been voted Premier League Manager of the Month twice. There was a minor misstep in October when they travelled to Old Trafford to renew old rivalries with Manchester United, Adam Lallana rescuing a point five minutes from time in a 1-1 draw to ensure that the side did not suffer their first league defeat since the loss to Manchester City in January. For such a fierce perfectionist like Klopp, the two dropped points was an irritation rather than disaster and the Reds were nonetheless six clear points of City in the table.

Between the end of October and the middle of December the Reds were remarkable as the side relentlessly hammered home their advantage. All eight fixtures brought victories, the most notable the 3-1 success against City at Anfield and a 5-2 derby triumph over Everton (Klopp's 100th win in the Premier League), but after beating Watford 2-0 on Merseyside, their 15th league triumph in 16 fixtures, Liverpool had to take another break from their quest for the title as they headed to the sunnier climes of Qatar for the FIFA Club World Cup. Previous English clubs competing in the competition had often seen it as a troublesome distraction from their principal focus of the Premier League but as the Reds boarded their plane to the Middle East, they were 10 points in front of Leicester City with the season almost at the halfway stage.

A capacity crowd of over 45,000 flocked to the Khalifa International Stadium in Doha to watch the side's semi-final clash with Monterrey. The Mexicans had booked their place in the tournament after winning the CONCACAF Cup, contested by the best sides in North and Central America and the Caribbean,

Klopp's 100th win in the Premier League.

The Reds boarded their plane to the Middle East.

ABOVE: Xherdan Shaqiri takes on Leonel Vangioni of Monterrey in the FIFA Club World Cup semi-final.

OPPOSITE: Manager and captain show mutual appreciation.

earlier in the year and proved themselves stubborn opposition. The game was level at 1-1 late on but was finally decided when Firmino, who had only been on the pitch for five minutes after replacing Origi, turned home Trent Alexander-Arnold's cross. The result capped a bizarre 24 hours for the club, coming just a day after a second-string Liverpool team coached by Under-23s manager Neil Critchley were beaten 5-0 away by Aston Villa in the quarter-finals of the League Cup over 3,000 miles away back in England. The starting XI may have been unfamiliar but despite losing, the team did make history as the youngest ever side Liverpool had ever fielded in a competitive fixture. The average age of Critchley's charges was 19 years and 182 days and there were five debutants on show. A 16-year-old Harvey Elliott made just his third senior appearance for the club in the match.

ABOVE: Naby Keita sees off a challenge from Vitinho of Flamengo in the FIFA Club World Cup final.

RIGHT: Firmino does it again for Liverpool.

OPPOSITE: Mutual appreciation continues.

Since it was first staged in 2000, the Reds had reached the final of the Club World Cup once before. They had lost 1-0 to São Paulo in 2005 and it was Brazilian opposition again 14 years later in the shape of Flamengo, the reigning South American club champions, in Doha. The final was a tense affair throughout with possession and attempts evenly shared and required extra-time to decide the destination of the silverware. Man of the Match Firmino was the hero for a second match in succession, scoring in the 99th minute with a cool finish and when the final whistle sounded, Liverpool were crowned the best club side on the planet.

> **Since it was first staged in 2000, the Reds had reached the final of the Club World Cup once before.**

MATCH STATS

FIFA CLUB WORLD CUP 2019

Saturday, 21 December 2019
(Khalifa International Stadium, Al Rayyan; attendance 45,416)

Liverpool (0) 1 – Flamengo (0) 0
(Firmino 99)

Liverpool: Alisson; Van Dijk, Robertson, Gomez, Alexander-Arnold, Henderson, Oxlade-Chamberlain (Lallana 75), Keïta (Milner 100), Firmino (Origi 105), Salah (Shaqiri 120), Mané.

For Klopp, victory gave the German another piece

Man of the Match Firmino was the hero for a second match in succession.

of history as the Reds first manager to conquer the world. "The boys dug in again and massively put in a performance," he said after the game. "They kept getting tested constantly, our life is like this. At the moment we pass test after test after test. We have to make sure we pass further tests as well. I struggle to find the words to express my respect for the boys. It was incredible. We did so many good things. It was a very intense game for different reasons, it was not our best game we have ever played but it was enough to win. This was a wonderful night for the club. I said before I didn't not know how it would feel. Now I know it feels outstanding, absolutely sensational."

The squad returned to Merseyside with Christmas just three days away. As ever the festive celebrations would have to be modest with a Boxing Day clash with Leicester at the King Power Stadium just around the corner but any fears the side's Middle East trip had taken too much out of them were spectacularly dispelled. The Foxes were still Liverpool's closest challengers at kick-off but the home side were comprehensively swept aside with two more goals from the red-hot Firmino in a 4-0 win.

Four back-to-back clean sheets followed in the next four victories, including defeats of both Spurs and Manchester United, and by late February and a 3-2 success against West Ham at Anfield, the Reds had played 27 times in the league and failed to win only once. The Hammers result restored the team's almost unbelievable 22-point advantage at the summit of the Premier League – Manchester City were now back into the second – and although there were 33 points still on offer, it was inconceivable Liverpool could be caught.

Four back-to-back clean sheets followed in the next four victories, including defeats of both Spurs and Manchester United.

Given their extraordinary form and a record-equalling 18 consecutive top-flight league victories, it was a seismic shock when the Reds were beaten 3-0 at Watford in their final game in February. The dream of an unbeaten Premier League campaign was shattered but the team dusted itself off quickly and took another unstoppable step towards the title the following week when they beat Bournemouth 2-1 at Anfield. The win was their 22nd successive success at home in the league, breaking the long-standing top-flight club record set under Bill Shankly in 1972.

Four days later Liverpool refocused on the defence of their Champions League crown and the crucial second leg of their Last 16 encounter with Atlético Madrid. Trailing 1-0 from the first game in Spain, the Reds sent the tie into extra-time at Anfield courtesy of a Georginio Wijnaldum header after 43 minutes. The additional half hour saw Firmino put the team 2-1 up on aggregate but there was heartbreak at the death as Atlético scored twice to snatch victory from the jaws of defeat on Merseyside and dramatically knock Liverpool out.

CELEBRATIONS DESPITE COVID

Forty-eight hours later, the Atlético result was suddenly put into sobering context. Since the start of 2020, fears about the global spread of the Coronavirus virus had been growing and news began to emerge that a number of clubs had confirmed cases of Covid-19 in their squads. The country was not yet in a nationwide lockdown but on March 13 the Premier League, along with the Football League and Women's Super League, took the unprecedented decision to halt all fixtures. The suspension was initially to last until early April but it would in fact be more than three months before Liverpool took to the field again.

"I don't think this is a moment where the thoughts of a football manager should be important, but I understand for our supporters they will want to hear from the team and I will front that," Klopp said as he and the club came to terms with the completely unexpected interruption to the season. "First and foremost, all of us have to do whatever we can do protect one another. In society, I mean. This should be the case all the time in life, but in this moment I think it matters more than ever. I've said before that football always seems the most important of the least important things. Today, football and football matches really aren't important at all.

"If it's a choice between football and the good of the wider society, it's no contest."

"Of course we don't want to play in front of an empty stadium and we don't want games and competitions suspended, but if doing so helps one individual stay healthy – just one – we do it, no questions. If it's a choice between football and the good of the wider society, it's no contest. Really, it isn't. Today's decision and announcement is being implemented with the motive of keeping people safe. Because of that we support it completely. We have seen members of teams we compete against become ill. This virus has shown that being involved in football offers no immunity. To our rival clubs and individuals who are affected and to those who later will become so, you are in our thoughts and prayers."

Football went into a surreal hibernation. Players were forced to train on their own in a bid to maintain their fitness but Klopp was in constant contact with his squad as they, the fans and the whole country

ABOVE: A lone figure. Not something Klopp was expecting during his Liverpool tenure – training during a worldwide pandemic during Covid restrictions.

struggled to come terms with the new reality of the pandemic. In his 2023 autobiography, *Sí Señor: My Liverpool Years*, Firmino revealed what life was like for the Liverpool players during the once-in-a-lifetime period of isolation. "We'll never forget March 2020, when everything changed," he wrote. "Everyone's lives became affected by the coronavirus pandemic. Many lost family members or loved ones. Defeat at Watford wasn't just the end of our unbeaten run. Looking at what happened afterwards, it also took away our chance to be champions before the pandemic forced a halt, denying us the opportunity to share that moment with our fans.

"When the authorities decided that football had to stop, we had a 25-point lead over Manchester

City with just 27 points left to play for. In other words, we were champions, but we weren't champions yet. There were even discussions about cancelling the league altogether, which made me nervous. Can you imagine? We'd had an extraordinary, epic campaign and they were going to deny us the title?

BELOW: Everton at an eerily empty Goodison Park, played host to Liverpool's first game since football was reinstated, following the coronavirus lockdown.

The club organised daily routines to keep everyone fit, morning yoga, afternoon training. All the players stayed connected via Skype, with the fitness coach overseeing and leading the training sessions. It was also a way to keep us connected and bonded. Liverpool arranged our supermarket shopping, we didn't have to do anything. I didn't pass my front gate in two months."

On 21 June, however, the beautiful game was

"Liverpool arranged our supermarket shopping."

back. There were no supporters inside Goodison Park to witness the strangest of all Merseyside derbies against Everton as a result of the stringent Covid protocols but it didn't really seem to matter. The game ended goalless but the point still took the Reds another inexorable step closer to the Premier League trophy they so badly craved.

Only three days later the team ran out at an empty Anfield. Crystal Palace were the visitors and despite the bizarre lack of crowd noise synonymous with the Kop, Liverpool played with the same intensity they had displayed throughout the season and stormed to victory. Goals from Alexander-Arnold and Salah in the first half were followed by strikes from Fabinho and Mané after the break and on the back of their 4-0 win, the Reds were just two points shy of the winning line. In such a wildly unpredictable season, it was perhaps unsurprising that Klopp's team did not

On 21 June however the beautiful game was back.

ABOVE: A haunting image of Klopp, surrounded by flags and empty seats at Anfield, where Liverpool were visited by Crystal Palace.

OPPOSITE: Joe Gomez fights for the ball with Jordan Ayew.

actually have to play again to wrap up the silverware as Manchester City were beaten 2-1 at Chelsea the next day to mathematically bring what had always been a one-horse title race to an end.

After three decades, the long wait to be crowned the champions of England for the 19th time was over. The enforced lack of fans, the absence of the traditional open top bus tour through the city and the strange backdrop to their triumph was not in the script but Klopp had delivered what every Liverpool supporter had dreamed of. He had said at his first press conference when he was unveiled to the media in 2015 that he didn't compare himself "to these genius managers in the history of Liverpool" but in winning the Premier League, the German had certainly joined that exclusive club.

The manager had gathered his players at a hotel to watch the City game and when the full time whistle blew, Klopp spoke to LFCTV and sent a message to the fans. "This is for you," he said. "It is wonderful to share it, but we share it with everybody out there as well because we are here, but we are all together. My message is, it is for you out there. It is really for you. I hope you feel it. I hope you saw it last night [against Palace], not only last night but after a long time, last night again. It is for so many people.

"I couldn't have dreamed of something like that and I never did before last year, honestly."

"I couldn't have dreamed of something like that and I never did before last year, honestly. We were

"This is for you," he said. "It is wonderful to share it."

not close enough three years ago, a year ago we were really close. What the boys have done in the last two-and-a-half years, the consistency they show is absolutely incredible and second to none. The boys love being part of this club, they love being part of the story of this club and the history. It is so nice how we learned how to deal with the history, how we learned to use the history in the last two years. It is just amazing."

The remaining seven league games of the season were largely irrelevant – four wins, two defeats and a draw – but Liverpool had already rewritten the record books. No side had ever won the top-flight title with so many fixtures to spare while the team's run of 24 league wins at home, straddled over two seasons, broke the previous English football record of 21 which the Reds had previously set. Their unbeaten season at Anfield – collecting a record 55 points – made it three league campaigns in a row they had not tasted defeated on their own patch for the first time in the club's history. Away from home their total of 44 points on the road in 2019-20 was a joint record, while 21 away games without losing was a standalone milestone.

Liverpool's haul of 79 from 81 points in their opening 27 matches made history, the best ever start to a league campaign in any of Europe's top five divisions. Their final tally of 32 Premier League triumphs matched the previous English record set by Manchester City in 2017-18 and 2018-19 and Tottenham back in 1919-20. They became the first side to win the title in eight different decades and were also the first club to hold the European Cup, European Super Cup, FIFA World Club Cup and Premier League at the same time.

There was one more curious statistic. The 85 goals Klopp's team scored was four less than they had registered in their previous campaign. The 33 goals they conceded was 10 more than the season before

ABOVE: An elated Klopp with the Premier League trophy.

RIGHT: Let's get the party started – dressing room antics and celebrations. The Reds enjoy the moment that Liverpool fans have been waiting years to finally experience.

and yet in 2018-19 they missed out on the silverware by a single point, while in 2019-20 they finished 18 full points clear of Manchester City.

Many members of the media discussed exactly how Klopp had masterminded his side's glorious achievement, transforming Liverpool from also-rans to champions, after they had lifted the Premier League trophy and the BBC's Phil McNulty arguably gave the greatest insight into the secrets of the German's success.

"Less than five years [after his appointment], no one doubts Klopp or his players," he wrote. "After a remarkable rise from 10th place on his arrival to European champions for the sixth time, they have now returned to their domestic perch as Premier League champions. Klopp's public persona is the big man with the tactile approach and the booming laugh. The animated presence in the technical area, celebrating with players and fans. So much more goes on behind the public image – so much more that gives the lie to those who nonsensically claimed Klopp's greatest coaching quality in his early days was as a cheerleader.

"Behind the scenes, away from the public gaze, his meticulous approach, as well as his intellect for football's modern methods and matters outside the game, make him the towering figure in Liverpool's spectacular revival. The notion that he simply strolls around Melwood smiling and hugging people may sustain those who wish to pour cold water on his brilliant successes, or downplay his tactical shrewdness. The reality could not be more different. Klopp believes the training ground is where the difference is made. This is where the drills are run through, where tactical ideas are tried and tested. Bolt onto this some spectacular recruitment and you have the 2019-20 Premier League champions.

After three decades, the long wait to be crowned the champions of England for the 19th time was over.

"Every session is meticulously planned with his staff before training. Klopp will then address his players to outline their work in depth. He is not just Liverpool's manager, he is Liverpool's coach. Every aspect of every day is plotted and analysed in minute detail. In preparing for games, he insatiably gathers information before condensing it into the essential and most urgent details. Inside Anfield this is regarded as a key skill that helps drive one of his best qualities – the ability to take big decisions quickly, without prevarication, and getting those decisions right.

"Klopp himself is the exact model of planning and efficiency he expects of others. He insists on punctuality, on everything operating like clockwork. If a meeting is planned for 10am, 10am it is. His and Liverpool's success is the result of a fiercely driven individual. There are no gimmicks. No 'Hollywood' moment was transformative in the story leading to Liverpool's coronation as Premier League champions. Klopp is the leader, strategist and inspiration. On the pitch, Klopp has earned his reputation alongside the other coaching greats now in the Premier League."

SOUNDS OF SILENCE (2020-21)

No supporters and no silverware made the 2020-21 campaign a testing one for Jürgen Klopp as the manager strived to emulate the incredible successes of the two previous seasons.

By the summer of 2020 Klopp had been in the managerial game for 19 years. Memories of the surreal celebrations following Liverpool's cathartic Premier League triumph, achieved against the backdrop of Covid-19, were still fresh given that the previous season had only finished in late July but the German was, as ever, firmly looking forward rather back. His near two decades in the dugout and the wealth of coaching experience he had accumulated would be put to the sternest of tests as the Reds readied themselves to mount their defence of their title.

The on-going pandemic both helped and hindered the manager's pre-season preparations. Global travel restrictions had prompted the decision to reluctantly postpone the summer's scheduled European Championships and the Olympics in Tokyo, including the men's football competition. This meant Klopp did not lose any of his squad to either tournament, a rarity for a manager in the modern era, but it was not all positive news. The same travel considerations meant

By the summer of 2020 Klopp had been in the managerial game for 19 years.

ABOVE: **Joel Matip of Liverpool leaps the tallest to score for the Reds against Blackpool in a pre-season friendly.**

Liverpool's options for pre-season fixtures were limited and it would be a significantly shortened build-up to the new campaign.

In recent previous summers the Reds had flown off to America to ready the players for a return to action but Klopp and his coaching had to content themselves with a training camp in Austria and friendlies against Stuttgart and Red Bull Salzburg. A game against Blackpool at Anfield in early September completed the pre-season programme but with no further fixtures – they had played seven pre-season friendlies 12 months earlier and nine the summer before – it was far from the extensive preparation that the manager was renowned for.

"As we know, Jürgen's teams play with intensity that is different to another manager," said Brazilian midfielder Lucas Leiva, a veteran of more than 300 games for the club and a player with insight having been part of the squad in Klopp's first ever preseason in the summer of 2016. "Competitiveness is inside every single player, so there's plenty of that during the preseason. Small-sided games and also in the running. Lots of running. Especially in the first 10 days, two weeks, I think it's the most difficult.

"Jürgen likes to work as after the preseason you don't have too much time to train, so it's a really important part of the season. Every session you can work tactically. Every session you can put in a little of the way you want to play, especially for the new players. Depending on what they do, they always try to put something in so that slowly they start to understand the way Jürgen wants to play."

There was not though a flood of 'new players' to learn the ropes after Liverpool had completed their transfer business. The two headline recruits were midfielder Thiago from Bayern Munich in a £20 million deal and the signing of striker Diogo Jota from Wolves for £41 million while Adam Lallana and Dejan Lovren both left the club. As he had done the previous summer, Klopp had resolved to place his trust principally in the same group of players and a squad which had just given him the greatest success of his managerial career.

ABOVE: Salah is put under pressure from Pascal Struijk of Leeds United in September 2020.

LEFT: Klopp prepares Diogo Jota for his Liverpool debut against Arsenal.

DEFENCE DECIMATED

Despite hopes that supporters may be allowed to return to stadia for the new season, Liverpool kicked off against Leeds United at Anfield in September to the disappointing sound of silence courtesy of Covid and the continuing ban on crowds. By now it was a familiar if frustrating dynamic for the players but the Reds still began in explosive style with a 4-3 win on Merseyside. The three points came in dramatic fashion despite Klopp's side taking the lead three

times, only to be pegged back each time by their visitors, and it required a late Mohamed Salah penalty two minutes from time to seal victory and complete what was the Egyptian's second Premier League hat-trick for the Reds.

Confidence-boosting wins over Chelsea and Arsenal followed but at the start of October the team experienced a defeat that sent shockwaves through the club. No one expected their trip to Aston Villa to be a foregone conclusion for the champions and no one predicted they would suffer a 7-2 hammering in Birmingham after an error-strewn display. It was the first time Liverpool had conceded seven times in a game since 1963 and was only the side's fourth league loss since the beginning of 2019.

"[We] lost the plot," admitted Klopp as he struggled to come to terms with what had unfolded at Villa Park. "I can't explain, I'm not sure, but I can tell you what

"[We] lost the plot," admitted Klopp as he struggled to come to terms with what had unfolded at Villa Park.

I saw. All their big moments led to a big chance or goal and that makes the difference. They were flying and we were open. All the things you should not do in a football match, we did tonight. They were very physical, very smart and very direct, we were not. We had big chances which we did not use, but when you concede seven I'm not sure you can say it would have been 7-7. We made too many mistakes and massive ones obviously. It started with the first goal and around the goals we made massive mistakes."

It was too early to panic but three days earlier the Reds had been knocked out of the League Cup, losing in the fourth round on penalties to Arsenal at Anfield, and with the Merseyside derby at Goodison next up, Klopp needed a response from the team. The manager got it in terms of performance with goals from Sadio Mané and Salah earning a point after a 2-2 draw, a result which extended Liverpool's unbeaten run against their city rivals to a record 23 games in all competitions.

Any joy at steadying the ship however was immediately tempered by an injury to Virgil van Dijk.

Any joy at steadying the ship however was immediately tempered by an injury to Virgil van Dijk.

The Dutch defender was hurt in a reckless challenge by Everton goalkeeper Jordan Pickford and forced off the pitch after only 11 minutes. It later emerged the centre-back had suffered a serious ACL injury

OPPOSITE: Jürgen receives his Best FIFA Men's Coach Award from Chief of Global Football Development Arsène Wenger.

BELOW: Everton's Jordan Pickford goes in with a wayward tackle resulting in serious injury for Virgil van Dijk.

"On behalf of my coaches, I accept it obviously."

which would require surgery and after just five league games, Klopp had lost his most influential defender for the rest of the campaign. Less than a month later, the German lost Joe Gomez to another season-ending injury. The defender ruptured a tendon in his left knee in a training session while on international duty with England and within the space of a few short weeks, the Reds had been cruelly shorn of two of their most important defensive players.

There was better news on the pitch and in late November the Reds beat Leicester City 3-0 at Anfield. The victory was their 64th unbeaten outing at home in the top flight, setting a new club record. The side's good form continued for the remainder of 2020 with three wins and four draws in the Premier League in November and December to leave the side top of the table before the New Year. December was a particularly good month for the German, including a 2-1 defeat of Spurs and 7-0 demolition of Crystal Palace, and five days before Christmas there was an early present for the manager when he was named the Coach of the Year at the BBC Sports Personality of the Year awards. Klopp became the eighth football manager to collect the accolade, following in the footsteps of the likes of Sir Alex Ferguson and Arsène Wenger, but the Reds boss was characteristically quick to heap praise on others for the award. "When the coach of the Team of the Year becomes the Coach of the Year, then I had an outstanding team on the pitch obviously," he said. "My coaching staff is obviously the main reason why all the things worked the way they work, so I'm really happy. On behalf of my coaches, I accept it obviously and take it home to Liverpool. Thank you very much."

Klopp's BBC prize came exactly 364 days after his team had beaten Brazilian side Flamengo 1-0 in Qatar to be crowned FIFA Club World Champions. It also came in the same week that the German was named the Best FIFA Men's Coach for a second successive year. There was understandable reason to celebrate in the Klopp household over Christmas but the first six months of 2021 were to prove the most difficult test of his Anfield reign to date.

ANFIELD WOES

The Reds began the New Year against Southampton at St Mary's. A 1-0 defeat on the South Coast, with old boy Danny Ings netting after just two minutes, was only their second in the league but it did mean the champions had collected just two points from a possible nine in their last three league matches. A 4-1 success win over Aston Villa in the third round of the FA Cup lifted the mood around Anfield briefly but the rest of January brought a series of setbacks from which the champions never fully recovered.

The visit of Burnley to Merseyside was billed as an opportunity for the team to rediscover their form in front of goal after drawing a blank in their previous two games, and scoring just once in the last four, but the Clarets hadn't read the script and a late winner from the spot from Ashley Barnes gave the visitors their first win at Anfield since 1974. More disappointingly, the defeat brought to an end Liverpool's unbeaten sequence at home in the Premier League after 68 matches – they had lost 1,370 days ago against Crystal Palace in April 2017 – and left the Reds six points adrift of the league leaders.

There was little time to lick their wounds and three days later they faced Manchester United in the FA Cup at Old Trafford. A double from Salah put some of the side's attacking woes behind them but it was frailties at the other end of the pitch which were pivotal and a 78th-minute free-kick gave the home side a 3-2 win.

A bad month then got worse. The side's 3-1 success against Tottenham in north London was a welcome return to winning ways after five fixtures without a victory but the result came at a price Liverpool could ill afford. Defender Joe Matip made

Eliminated from both domestic cup competitions and embroiled in a fierce fight for a top four finish, the Reds now had to solider on without their three first-choice centre-backs.

it through to half-time but did not emerge from the dressing room for the second 45 and it was later confirmed he had sustained an ankle ligament injury against Spurs that would keep him out for the rest of the season. Eliminated from both domestic cup

competitions and embroiled in a fierce fight for a top four finish, the Reds now had to soldier on without their three first-choice centre-backs.

It was a challenge their diminished defensive resources could not meet. The aura of fortress Anfield through February and early March disappeared, not least because of the empty seats in the stadium, and Klopp's team suffered six successive league losses at home. Before the last of the six, against Fulham,

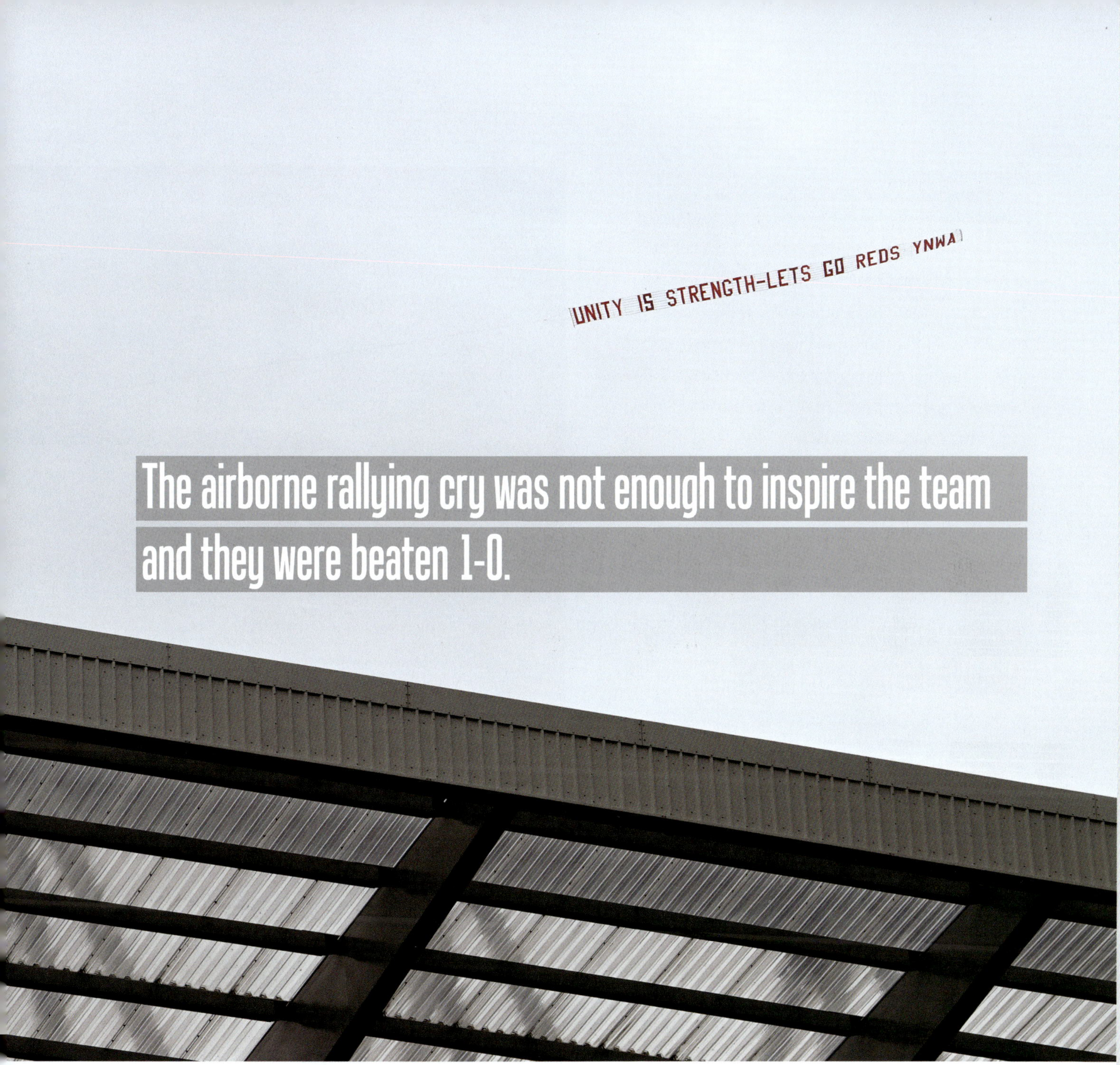

The airborne rallying cry was not enough to inspire the team and they were beaten 1-0.

ABOVE: Inspiration for the Reds in the form of a banner.

a plane soared over Anfield displaying a banner reading 'Unity in Strength – Let's Go Reds YNWA' but the airborne rallying cry was not enough to inspire the team and they were beaten 1-0. The result saw the Reds slip down into eighth in the table and looking a shadow of the side that had swept aside all their rivals the previous season.

RETURN OF THE REAL REDS

It's often said that adversity reveals a side's true character and mired in what was undoubtedly their biggest crisis since Klopp had become manager, Liverpool displayed a collective resolve that ultimately saved their season. There were 10 league fixtures remaining following the Fulham defeat and the Reds valiantly rallied to ensure they were unbeaten in all of them. A 2-1 victory over Aston Villa

RIGHT: Supporters got to watch Liverpool play at Anfield at last after Covid laws were paired back, albeit socially distanced and adorned with masks.

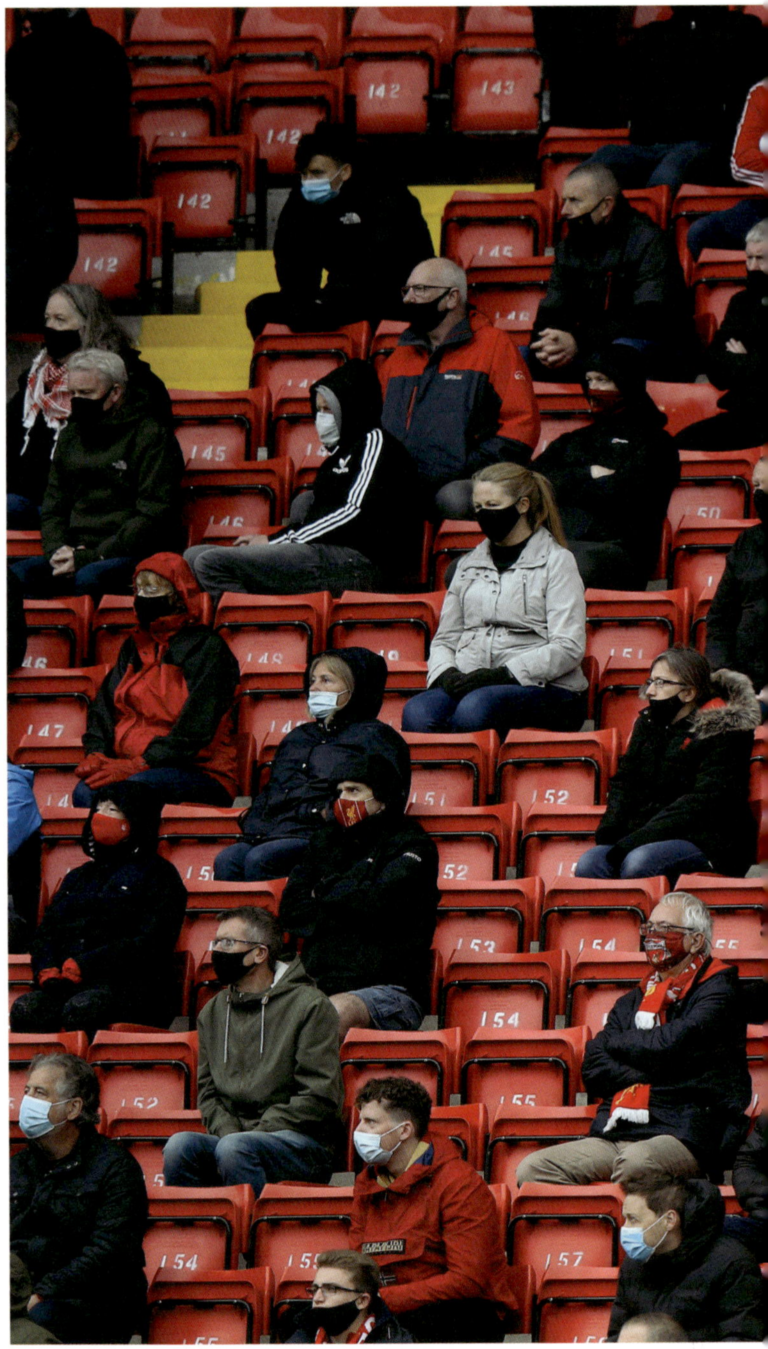

in April put to bed their recent problems at Anfield while a dramatic and historic winner from Alisson in the 95th minute against West Brom at the Hawthorns in May, the first time a goalkeeper had ever scored for Liverpool in a competitive game, took the Reds up to fifth with two matches to play.

A 3-0 success against Burnley in their penultimate fixture, avenging the defeat at Anfield in January, elevated the team into the top four on goal difference above Leicester. Three points meant the Reds' hopes

A match watched by 10,000 fans after the belated relaxation of the Covid rules, the side ensured there were no mistakes with an assured 2-0 win.

of Champions League qualification were in their own hands and in their final game against Crystal Palace at Anfield, a match watched by 10,000 fans after the belated relaxation of the Covid rules, the side ensured there were no mistakes with an assured 2-0 win. Both goals came from Mané as the Kop celebrated for the first time since March 2020 while Klopp breathed a quiet sigh of relief.

"A top-four spot looked beyond Liverpool when they sat eighth in early March after a campaign undermined by injuries and a catastrophic run of home form including six successive Anfield league defeats," reported *BBC Sport*. "Even at the end of April, they remained four points off fourth place with just five games to go but won each of those to not only seal a place at Europe's top table again but also leapfrog Chelsea into third."

Even the manager himself was surprised that his side had successfully salvaged the season from the wreckage of their results immediately after Christmas. "Finishing the season in third is incredible," he said. "We wanted this feeling, this game, this atmosphere. Credit to the boys, I can't believe how

"Finishing the season in third is incredible."

it worked out in the last few weeks. Incredible. If someone told me five, six, eight weeks ago we can finish the season in third, it was out of reach, barely possible. Fighting through this is the best lesson you could learn in life. From nowhere to the Champions League in five weeks is a massive achievement."

Given that Van Dijk, Gomez and Matip had played only 26 times in the Premier League between them, that achievement was even greater and although Liverpool had been dethroned as champions of England, their late revival when it really mattered proved that the uncharacteristic midseason slump

for Klopp and his side was merely temporary rather than a sign of long-term decline.

EUROPEAN ELIMINATION

Liverpool's 2020-21 Champions League challenge was not a vintage one by the club's lofty European standards but it still took the might of then 13-time champions Real Madrid to stop Klopp's side in its tracks. Drawn in the group stage against Ajax, Atalanta and Danish minnows Midtjylland, the Reds did the bulk of the heavy lifting required in their opening three matches, scoring eight and conceding none, to claim nine points from nine and although their serene progress to the knockout phase was briefly threatened after a 2-0 defeat to Atalanta at Anfield in late November, the team went safely through as group winners.

They were equally untroubled in the Last 16 against RB Leipzig. The Germans were unable to shackle the attacking threat of either Salah or Mané over the two legs, both players scoring home and away, and the Reds coasted to a 4-0 aggregate triumph.

The first leg of the quarter-final in April took Liverpool to the Bernabeu for their showdown with Madrid. Forced to field a makeshift centre-half pairing

"We didn't lose the tie tonight, we lost in Madrid."

LEFT: Salah scores for Liverpool in their Champions League quarter-final match with Real Madrid at the Bernabeu. Liverpool eventually lost out to the Spanish giants.

of Nat Phillips and on-loan Ozan Kabak, the Reds were on the backfoot for much of the match in Spain but

The Reds were on the backfoot for much of the match in Spain but trailing 2-0, were given hope when Salah struck in the 51st minute.

trailing 2-0, were given hope when Salah struck in the 51st minute. Real however scored again to seal a 3-1 win and with eight days to prepare for the return fixture on Merseyside, Klopp and his team were in need of another magical night at Anfield and one of their trademark European comebacks.

It did not materialise. Salah, James Milner and Georginio Wijnaldum all had first-half chances which had they been converted could have sowed seeds of doubt in the ranks of the Spanish visitors but they didn't go in and Liverpool were repeatedly repelled. The game finished goalless, propelling Madrid into the last four, while Klopp was left to reflect on spurned opportunities. "We didn't lose the tie tonight, we lost in Madrid," he admitted. "You always need the key moments. It was uncomfortable for Madrid. We were good, aggressive, had chances. We didn't score and then the experience of Real Madrid played the tie down. That is ourselves this year with the finishing."

The side's strong form at the business end of the Premier League went some way to easing the pain of their Champions League exit but 2020-21 was nonetheless a chastening reality check after the Reds' record-breaking feats of the previous season. "Liverpool failed to retain their Premier League title but did manage to pull a Champions League qualification spot out of the bag when all had, for a time, looked lost," wrote Caoimhe O'Neill in her review of the campaign for *The Athletic*. "The injury crisis felt never-ending and even hindered the progress made by new signings Diogo Jota and Thiago. Curtis Jones enjoyed a breakthrough season and for all the talk of Trent Alexander-Arnold's struggles, the right-back found his best form to end the season in style. Liverpool's finishing was frustratingly lacking at times, but Salah held his own to score consistently – and, more often than not, to do it emphatically with that gifted left foot. In doing so, he has become the first Liverpool player to score 20 goals or more in three different Premier League seasons."

GOING THE DISTANCE (2021-22)

Two more major trophies, a third Champions League final and an unforgettable title race, 2021-22 was an epic season as Jürgen Klopp and his tireless team fought to make history.

Complaints about fixture congestion, player fatigue and the demands of incessant travel are a common refrain from managers in the modern era. Such familiar gripes often emanate from the coaches who are not in the hunt for silverware, rather than their touchline rivals with realistic prospects of lifting trophies, proving an adage that there is simply no such thing as too many games if there are medals at the end of the footballing rainbow. Tiredness is only a state of mind when you are

The Reds' relentless efforts earned the club three final appearances.

LEFT: Klopp arrives at Anfield, still taking the necessary Covid precautions.

winning big matches on the biggest stages.

Klopp certainly would not have been disappointed if he had known ahead of the 2021-22 season, his seventh at the helm, that his team would play every game possible over the course of an exhausting but exhilarating campaign that began on 14 August and lasted until 28 May. The physical demands of his squad playing a total of 63 times across four competitions were of course extreme but there is no gain without pain and the team's eye-watering workload was the welcome result of remarkable performances on the pitch.

The Reds' relentless efforts earned the club three final appearances and a dramatic battle for the Premier League title, which only reached its climax on the final day of the season. Over the course of all their 63 energy-sapping outings over 10 arduous months, Liverpool were in contention for an unprecedented quadruple. No English side has ever completed the fabled but elusive feat, nor any club from Europe's other 'top five' leagues in Spain, Germany, Italy or France, but 2021-22 was the year when Klopp came agonisingly close to masterminding what would have been the greatest season in the beautiful game's history.

There was though no sense of failure when Liverpool were ultimately denied the clean sweep. Two triumphs in three finals at Wembley, becoming the first club ever to secure the domestic cup double in England for a second time, was a historic achievement and although the league and then Europe brought heartbreak in the end, the team's 'heavy metal' displays were a thrilling reflection of the manager's all-encompassing philosophy and his commitment to entertain, as well as his players' remarkable stamina and style.

OLD TRAFFORD ONSLAUGHT

A reassuring sense of normality returned to football ahead of 2021-22. The Reds' preseason was restored to its former glory with a full compliment of nine friendlies (in which they were beaten just once) while the Premier League was once again scheduled to start in the middle of August in contrast to last season's delayed September kick-off. More significantly, the fans had been given the green light to return to Anfield and beyond in full force and with crowds back in stadia, the sense of anticipation for a new season unaffected by the pandemic was palpable.

The club made just one signing in the summer window. Admittedly it was a significant one, with the Reds investing £36 million to prise French central defender Ibrahima Konaté away from RB Leipzig, but Klopp was unconcerned about the relative inactivity in the transfer market. Virgil van Dijk, Joel Matip and Joe Gomez had all recovered from the injuries that had blighted them the previous season and with his defensive options restored to full strength, and Konaté added to the mix, the manager could begin his four-pronged assault on silverware.

Both Van Dijk and Matip returned to the heart of the Reds' defence in the starting XI for the Premier League opener against Norwich City at Carrow Road

Both Van Dijk and Matip returned to the heart of the Reds' defence.

– Gomez and Konaté were both on the bench – and Liverpool's marathon campaign began without undue alarm. Goals from Diogo Jota, Roberto Firmino and Mohamed Salah wrapped up a 3-0 win and in scoring the Egyptian wrote himself once again into

Salah was their tormentor in chief with a sensational hat-trick.

ABOVE: Salah was on the rampage at Manchester United, terrorising the Devils on his way to a deserved hat-trick.

OPPOSITE: Punching the air, Jürgen can't contain his delight at beating the old foes, Manchester United.

the club's history books by becoming the first Red to net on the opening day of a Premier League season for a fifth successive year.

It was a result which boded well for the extensive challenges ahead and sparked a nine-match unbeaten run in the league that signalled Liverpool meant business. The highlight of the statement sequence came in late October when Klopp took the team to Manchester to face United, just five months after they had left Old Trafford on the back of a 4-2 victory. Their return to the home of their fiercest rivals was irrepressible and Salah was their tormentor in chief with a sensational hat-trick. It was the 10th game in a row he was on target while Liverpool's 5-0 demolition of United was a record scoreline at Old Trafford.

"Liverpool were always going to come back stronger from the suffering of last season, when injuries and the worst run of home form in the club's history saw them drawn into a dogfight for a place

The League Cup was a trophy that had so far eluded Klopp.

in the Champions League," wrote Phil McNulty for the *BBC Sport* website. "They rallied superbly to finish third and carried that good form into this new campaign, with an ominous composure about Klopp's side from the first day. With Virgil van Dijk back in defence and Salah playing at a level that suggests he is the world's best player, they are a ruthless machine and how United felt that power. With Salah as the main weapon, they cut through United at will, reducing both their players and the crowd to nervous agitation every time they went forward. Salah is in the form of his life and this United defence was an open invitation to him and Liverpool's range of attacking options."

Further standout results followed. A 4-0 drubbing of Arsenal at Anfield and their 4-1 triumph in the Merseyside derby at Goodison at the start of December in particular notable and although there were two defeats before the New Year, on the road to West Ham and Leicester, Liverpool's league form instilled a belief that was seamlessly translated into both their performances and results in the League Cup and Champions League.

KNOCKOUT PROGRESS

The League Cup was a trophy that had so far eluded Klopp during his reign on Merseyside. Liverpool had lifted the trophy a joint record eight times ahead of their 2021-22 challenge but it had been a decade since their last success in the competition and mindful of both, the manager selected a strong side for their

ABOVE: Luis Díaz in action for Porto. His appearances for the Portuguese side in the Champions League drew attention.

OPPOSITE: Conor Bradley makes his mark in the Liverpool team playing Norwich City in September 2021.

first assignment, away to Norwich in September. As ever though, the German had one eye on the future and the next generation of Liverpool stars and handed 18-year-old Northern Ireland defender Conor Bradley his senior debut. The Canaries were despatched 3-0 in a repeat of the league result at Carrow Road and after beating Preston North End and then Leicester on penalties, the Reds found themselves safely through to the semi-finals.

That was for early 2022 however and, beginning in September, the Champions League now took centre stage. AC Milan, Porto and Atlético Madrid stood between Liverpool and a place in the knockout stages and although it was a group of real quality, the Reds made a mockery of their rivals' European reputations with six wins from six. Their opener against Milan at Anfield was a thriller from which they emerged 3-2 winners thanks to skipper Jordan Henderson's second-half strike while it was the same scoreline in their favour against Atlético at the Wando Metropolitano in October courtesy of a Salah double in the Spanish capital. The Egyptian's pivotal double took his tally for the club in the Champions League to 31, eclipsing Steve Gerrard's previous record of 30. The remainder of the group stage was a procession as Klopp's side scored a total of 17 and conceded only six goals en route to the Last 16.

It had been a near-perfect first half of the season in 2023 – just two defeats in 29 games across three competitions – but once again Klopp was not willing to rest on his laurels. His side had scored 72 times in those 29 fixtures suggesting his attacking options, prolifically spearheaded by Salah, Sadio Mané, Jota and Firmino, were in rude health but the manager had already realised he would not be able to rely on his forward players forever despite their superb recent form. Recruitment from a position of strength rather in an emergency is always preferable and in January Liverpool signed Luis Díaz from Porto after the Colombian had impressed in both of his

Champions League appearances against the Reds. At 25, the forward cost the club a potential £49 million depending on appearances and performance targets but having added to his defence in the summer with the addition of the 22-year-old Konaté, Klopp had now begun his prudent plan to future-proof the attacking end of his squad.

KELLEHER THE HERO

The period from the start of January through to early April was hectic but mesmeric from the Reds on all four fronts as their campaign continued to gather momentum. Ten successive victories in the Premier League, starting with the 3-0 defeat of Brentford on Merseyside and ending with a 2-0 win over Watford, emphatically underlined Liverpool's title credentials and by the time they came to face Manchester City, it was evident that the champions would be one of the two sides playing at the Etihad. The game would not be definitive but it was certainly a clash between the two best teams in the division by a distance. Liverpool went behind twice but first Jota and then Mané, on his 30th birthday, restored parity. The striker's equaliser came in the 46th minute and to the surprise of everyone, there were no more goals and it finished 2-2. The result saw City stay above the Reds by a solitary point and with seven league fixtures remaining, the final destination of the Premier League trophy remained unclear.

In the Champions League, the march of Klopp's team also continued. Italians Inter Milan were disposed of in the Last 16 after a 2-1 aggregate victory, although Liverpool were beaten in the second leg at Anfield to end their seven-match-winning streak in the competition, and while the number of goals conceded in his side's 6-4 win over Benfica over two legs in the quarter-finals clearly frustrated the manager, their place in the last four was never in doubt.

Their run in the FA Cup was equally convincing in the first four rounds of action and the first serious test of their prospects of lifting the trophy came in the

Their run in the FA Cup was equally convincing in the first four rounds of action.

semi-finals in mid-March against City at Wembley. The match came just six days after the stalemate in the league at the Etihad but in what was the proverbial game of two halves, there was a winner this time. An irresistible first-half display from the Reds saw them draw first blood with a Konaté header followed by a double from Mané but City rallied after the break and scored twice, forcing Klopp's side to dig deep defensively and close out a famous 3-2 success. "Liverpool's victory," reported *Sky Sports* after the triumph in north London, "jubilantly celebrated by the red-shirted fans who made the trip to a sun-drenched Wembley, ends City's treble hopes and keeps their own dream of a quadruple alive."

That quadruple was still firmly in their sights courtesy of Liverpool's unstoppable progress in the League Cup. Their two-legged semi-final against Arsenal in January may have hung in the balance after a goalless draw at Anfield but despite both Mané and Salah being absent on Africa Cup of Nations duty, the Reds were ruthless in the return fixture in the capital and it was Jota who stepped up with two goals at the Emirates to secure the club's first appearance in a Wembley final for six years.

OPPOSITE: Celebrations for Mané, scoring against Manchester City in the FA Cup semi-final.

BELOW: Klopp has a big smile after Liverpool defeated Arsenal in the League Cup semi-final.

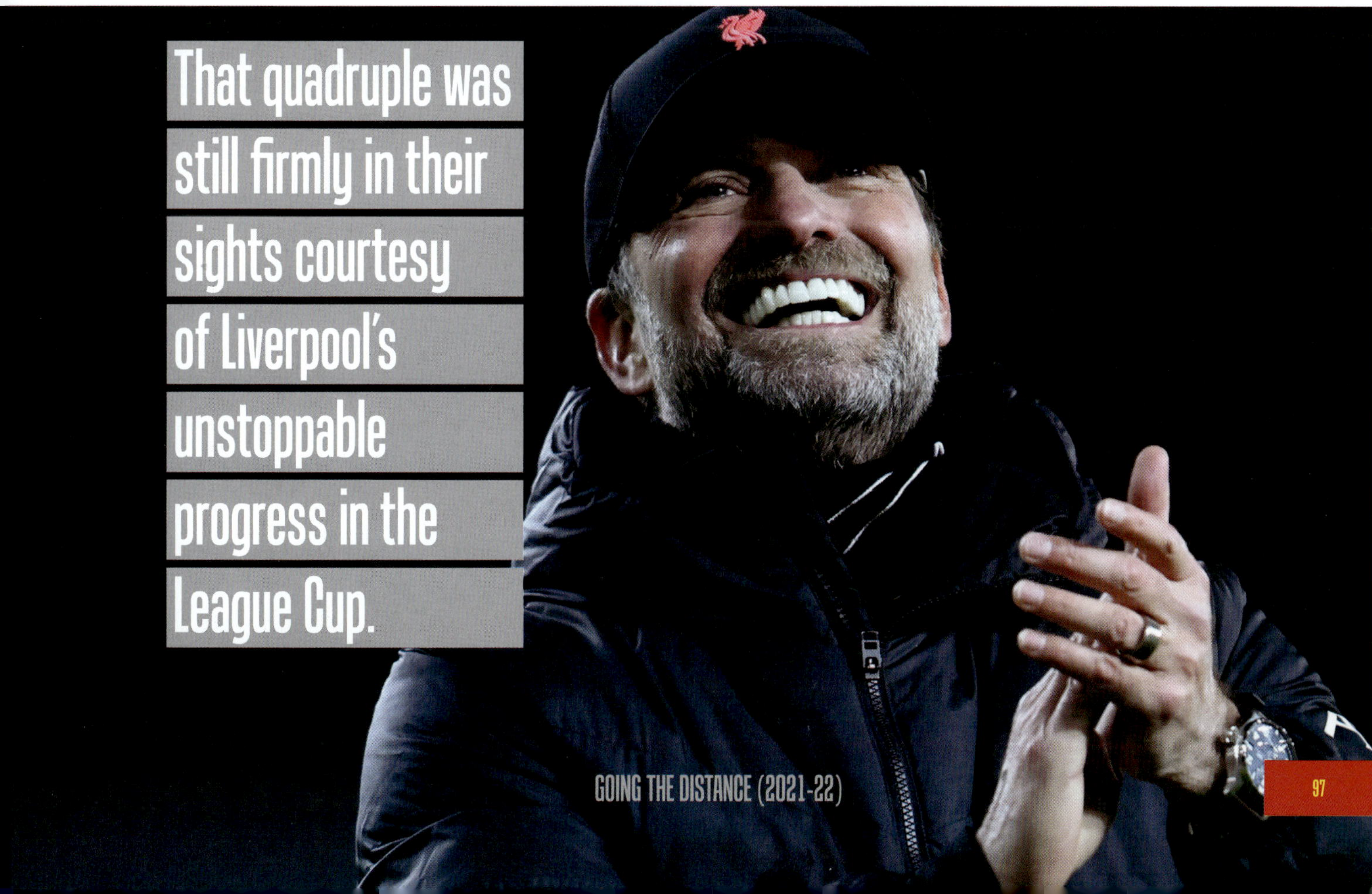

That quadruple was still firmly in their sights courtesy of Liverpool's unstoppable progress in the League Cup.

MATCH STATS

CARABAO CUP FINAL 2022

Sunday, 27 February 2022
(Wembley Stadium, London; attendance 85,512)

Liverpool (0) 0 – Chelsea (0) 0 (aet)
Liverpool won 11–10 on penalties

Liverpool: Kelleher; Alexander-Arnold, Matip (Konaté 91), Van Dijk, Robertson, Henderson (Elliott 79), Fabinho, Keïta (Milner 80), Salah, Mané (Jota 80), Díaz (Origi 97).

Making the right selections for the biggest games is when great managers distinguish themselves from the rest and ahead of February's showdown with Chelsea, Klopp was presented with a significant dilemma. Young Republic of Ireland goalkeeper Caoimhín Kelleher had started three of the club's League Cup fixtures en route to Wembley, including the crucial second leg defeat of the Gunners in the semis, but the manager now had to decide whether to keep faith with the 23-year-old or reinstate his first-choice keeper Alisson in the starting XI. In the end it was Kelleher who proudly lined up at the home of football for kick-off.

The final finished goalless after 90 minutes and then the half hour of extra time but the scoreline did not reflect what was a scintillating encounter and one which was ultimately decided by the three goalkeepers on show. Both sides had a succession of chances but Kelleher repelled Chelsea at every turn, most memorably with a crucial block at the near post in the dying seconds of the additional 30 minutes. His opposite number Edouard Mendy was equally inspired at the other end to keep a clean sheet of his own and the final went to a penalty shootout.

Chelsea manager Thomas Tuchel had by this time taken the decision to replace Mendy with Kepa Arrizabalaga, based on a reputation for his penalty-saving prowess, but neither the Spanish stopper nor Kelleher could do anything about the first 20 spot kicks as both Liverpool and the Blues nailed their efforts

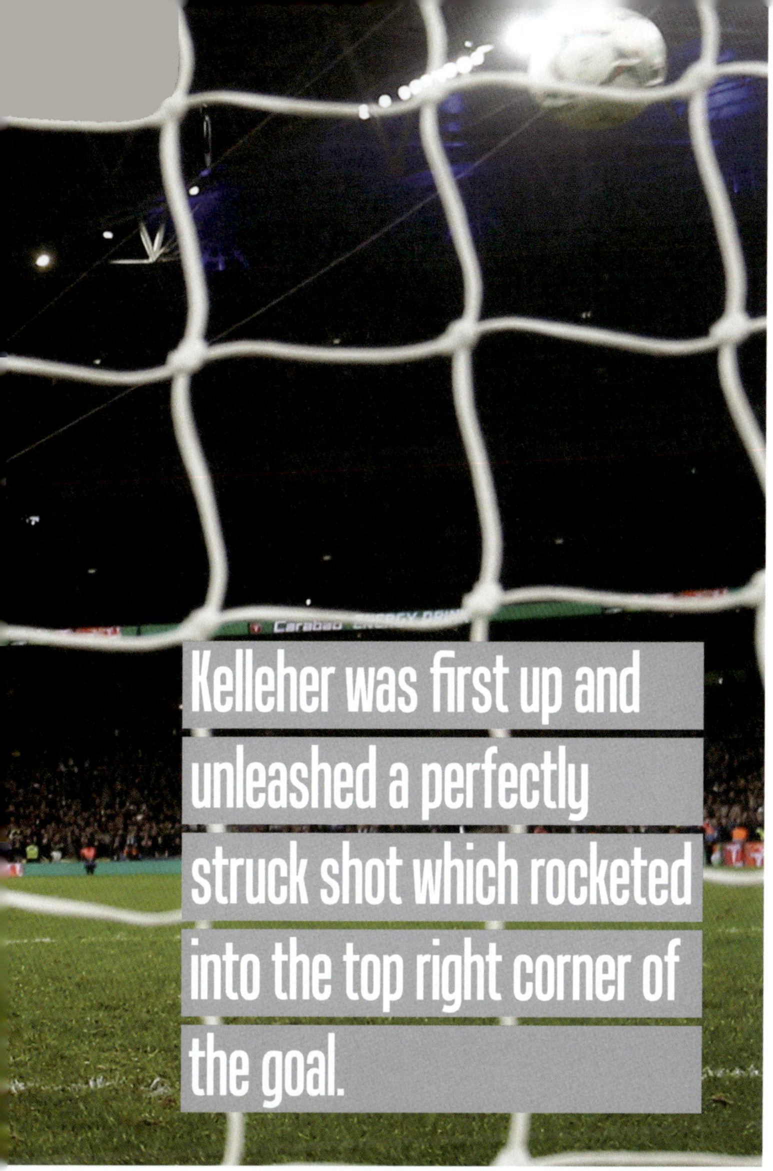

> Kelleher was first up and unleashed a perfectly struck shot which rocketed into the top right corner of the goal.

and remarkably it was 10-10 and with all the outfield players having successfully stepped up, it was time for the goalkeepers to make the dreaded, lonely walk to the penalty spot. Kelleher was first up and unleashed a perfectly struck shot which rocketed into the top right corner of the goal. There was no time to celebrate as he composed himself to face Arrizabalaga's penalty seconds later and he watched ecstatically as the Chelsea player blasted over the bar.

> Liverpool become the first side to lift the League Cup for a ninth time.

The Republic international's Man-of-the-Match display saw Liverpool become the first side to lift the League Cup for a ninth time. It was the fifth trophy of Klopp's career at Anfield and after the final whistle and the famous walk up the Wembley steps by the

LEFT: Liverpool keeper Kelleher displays some impressive spot kick skills to take his side onto victory against Chelsea.

BELOW: Klopp can hardly contain himself with excitement after victory over Chelsea.

"I am two things, a professional manager and a human being."

team to collect the silverware, the German was inevitably asked whether it had a been a difficult decision to pick Kelleher. His reply underlined that great managers are as often dictated by emotion as they are logic. "Even in professional football there should be space for some sentiment," he admitted. "Caoimhín Kelleher is a young boy, plays in all the competition, what do I do? I am two things, a professional manager and a human being and the human being won. He deserves it. At the training centre we have a wall that all goalkeepers are on who won something and Caoimhín can go on it – that's how it should be – absolutely great."

WEMBLEY DOUBLE

If the Liverpool faithful believed they had good reason to celebrate after their team's Wembley triumph, there was cause for a citywide party at the end of April. Just a day after the Reds had beaten Villarreal 2-0 at Anfield in the first leg of their Champions League semi-final, the news broke that Klopp had extended his contract with the club for a third time since he had arrived in 2015. His previous deal had been due to expire in the summer of 2024 but the German had now put pen to paper to add a further two years to the agreement. His trusted assistant managers Pep Lijnders and Peter Krawietz were also rewarded with improved contracts and as the season neared what would be a dramatic conclusion, everything on the touchline was in place for the immediate and longer-term challenges ahead.

"This is the news all Liverpool fans had been dreaming of, but more in hope than expectation with Klopp always adamant he would not extend his stay

That ongoing pursuit of silverware continued first with the FA Cup final in May.

at Anfield beyond 2024," wrote *Sky Sports'* Richard Morgan. "And the reason for the U-turn? Well, while

> "This is the news all Liverpool fans had been dreaming of."

Klopp claimed it was all down to his wife, Ulla, giving the move her blessing, which will no doubt have played an important part in his decision, it will mainly be down to this extraordinary team he has now built at Liverpool and the trophies they could yet still win.

"Maybe the thought of someone else coming to replace him and gaining the benefits of all his hard work was too much for him to bear. Klopp had always insisted he would continue as long as he had the energy to give such a demanding role his full focus, and as long as his trusted coaching team remained with him. Now let's see if the team can respond to his demand they must win more trophies to be considered one of the club's greatest ever."

That ongoing pursuit of silverware continued first with the FA Cup final in May. Chelsea were again the

ABOVE: **A proud moment for Jürgen, as he leads the team out onto the Wembley hallowed turf, for the FA Cup final.**

OPPOSITE: **Klopp signs on for another two years, as Liverpool fans take a collective sigh of relief.**

MATCH STATS

THE EMIRATES FA CUP FINAL 2022

Saturday, 14 May 2022
(Wembley Stadium, London; attendance 84,897)

Liverpool (0) 0 – Chelsea (0) 0 (aet)
Liverpool won 6–5 on penalties

Liverpool: Alisson; Alexander-Arnold, Konaté, Van Dijk (Matip 91), Robertson (Tsimikas 111), Keïta (Milner 74), Henderson, Thiago, Salah (Jota 33), Mané, Díaz (Firmino 98).

LEFT: Alisson proves his worth, crucially saving a penalty from Mason Mount of Chelsea in the FA Cup final shootout.

Alisson guessed right against Mason Mount, thrusting a strong left arm to beat out the shot.

opponents at Wembley but the crucial difference for the rematch in London was Klopp's decision to start with Alisson rather than Kelleher. It proved to be another inspired move as the Brazilian emulated his Irish team-mate with a crucial save in the shootout that secured a superb domestic cup double.

Liverpool twice hit the woodwork in the final through Díaz and Andy Robertson. They lost Salah to injury in the first half while Van Dijk did not return to the pitch after the initial 90 minutes but despite the near-misses and fitness setbacks, the Reds dominated possession and created more attempts on goal and were the unluckier of the two teams to be facing the lottery of penalties for the second time in the space of three months.

The shootout took its first twist when skipper Cesar Azplicueta slammed Chelsea's second spot kick against the post.

The shootout took its first twist when skipper Cesar Azplicueta slammed Chelsea's second spot kick against the post. James Milner, Thiago, Firmino and Trent Alexander-Arnold were not as wasteful with their penalties and as Mané readied himself to take the Reds' fifth, the Senegalese had the chance to win it. Hope turned to disappointment when Mendy saved but Mané's dejection quickly became joy when Alisson guessed right against Mason Mount, thrusting a strong left arm to beat out the shot. It now all rested on the shoulders Kostas Tsimikas and while many in the red half of Wembley could not bear to watch, the Greek full-back showed incredible nerve and calmly sent Mendy the wrong way to seal it 6-5 from 12 yards.

It's often said great managers are also lucky managers.

For the first time, Klopp had won the world's oldest cup competition and in doing so completed the German's remarkable collection of all three major English titles and Europe's elite tournament with Liverpool. It was the club's first FA Cup triumph in 16 years and their eighth overall while their domestic cup double in 2021-22 emulated Gérard Houllier's achievement in 2000-01 and made the Reds the only club ever to win the FA and League Cup in the same season twice.

It's often said great managers are also lucky managers. Klopp's selection of Alisson was more judgment than good fortune but the footballing gods were still looking favourably down on the Liverpool boss at Wembley. "The manager asked me which [penalty] number I want," Tsimikas revealed after the game when asked how the Reds' line-up on the spot had been decided. "He asks me 'who so far?' I say I want number seven. [He gave it to me] and number seven gave me the opportunity to win the game."

OPPOSITE: Never letting go – Jürgen lovingly cradles the newly acquired FA Cup on the flight back to Merseyside.

BELOW: Kostas Tsimikas delights his team and the Liverpool crowd with his winning penalty.

A BRIDGE TOO FAR

By the time the fans had abandoned Wembley for the bright lights of the capital and the FA Cup was safely nestled in the trophy cabinet at Anfield, there were three Premier League games to play. Neither Liverpool nor City had blinked as the title race intensified with each successive game – they were both unbeaten since their meeting in April – and when the Mancunians were held to a 2-2 draw at West Ham in

their penultimate fixture, coupled with the Reds' 2-1 victory at Southampton two days later, it came down to the final weekend of matches and the single point more than Liverpool that City had amassed over 37 games.

The task for Klopp's team was simple but ultimately unsatisfactory. Beat Wolves at Anfield and hope at the same time City were ambushed by Aston Villa at the Etihad. Liverpool fans never wavered in their belief in the build-up that Steven Gerrard would once again come to their rescue, this time in his role as the Villa manager rather than in the heart of the Reds' midfield, but even the former idol of the Kop was unable to prevent the season climaxing in the cruellest fashion.

For the first time, Klopp had won the world's oldest cup competition.

Liverpool made no mistake on Merseyside. A third-minute Wolves goal wasn't in the script but once Mané had levelled up, the anxiety that had been stifling the stadium receded and late second-half goals from Salah and Robertson ensured the three points were securely in the bag. The news from the Etihad that City had gone 2-0 down against Villa sent electric waves of hope through Anfield and although it was 2-1 after 76 minutes, had the scoreline stood Liverpool were champions. Two more goals for City, however, completed their fightback and Klopp's side were dramatically denied. 'You'll Never Walk Alone' rang around Anfield after the final whistle but rather than the celebratory song the fans had dreamed of it was a defiant refrain.

In 24 of the previous 29 seasons, the Reds' incredible haul of 92 points would have been enough to win the title.

In 24 of the previous 29 seasons, the Reds' incredible haul of 92 points would have been enough to win the title. Beaten only twice in 38 Premier League games, their tally was the third highest in the club's history and as just as he had at the end of 2018-19 when his team accumulated 97 points in the league with no trophy to show for their efforts, Klopp was left to contemplate what more he or his players could have done. Despite his own obvious dejection, he was characteristically as magnanimous in defeat as in victory. "Congratulations, first and foremost, to Man City, Pep Guardiola, all his staff and everybody from City for winning a tough race," he said. "That's how it is. If you want to win big, you have to be ready to lose big. We lost big today, not the game, but the league. The mood is obviously very, very disappointed."

Six days was all Klopp and his coaches had between the Wolves game and the Champions League final to reinvigorate their players physically and mentally for their showdown against Real Madrid in the Stade de France and a fixture seeped in illustrious European football history. It was the third time the two giants had met in the final, the first time in 1981 and most recently in 2018 when Madrid had run out 3-1 winners, and it was also the third time in Klopp's Liverpool reign that he had taken the team all the way to the highest-profile game in global club football.

Kick-off in the French capital was delayed by 30 minutes as the Liverpool faithful struggled to gain access to the ground as a result of the

No less than six times Salah was denied by Thibaut Courtois in the Spanish goal.

heavy-handed behaviour of the Parisian police and problems at the turnstiles. When the game did finally begin, the Reds were quickly in the ascendency in terms of both possession and attempts on goal and after 90 minutes had unleashed 24 shots on goal, nine on target, compared to just four efforts from Madrid. No less than six times Salah was denied by Thibaut Courtois in the Spanish goal, who also acrobatically tipped a Mané strike onto the post, and despite the pressure they could not find a way past an inspired goalkeeper. In cruel contrast Real's meagre two shots on target over 90 minutes produced the only, heartbreaking goal of the night

LEFT: A tantalisingly frustrating game for Liverpool against a lacklustre Real Madrid side in the Champions League final. None more so than Mo Salah, who was denied by keeper Courtois once again.

when Vinicius Jr beat Alisson on the hour mark.

It would have been understandable had Klopp faced the media post match with the demeanour of a manager who had been denied the victory his side's performance deserved but instead optod to remain optimistic. "Where is it next?" he asked the press, referring to the next Champions League final in 12 months time. "Istanbul? Book a hotel," he added in a defiant message to the fans.

BOOM AND BUST (2022-23)

A year of spectacular goal-laden victories as well as setbacks, 2022-23 saw Liverpool entertain and frustrate in equal measure.

To describe the 2021-22 campaign as an extended and emotional rollercoaster for the Reds and the supporters would be an understatement. The sheer length of the epic season ensured the joy and heartbreak it brought were felt even more keenly and when Klopp and his players decamped for the summer in the wake of the Champions League final, recharging mentally was as important as their physical recovery. There were just two short months

It was impossible to dismiss the Community Shield as little more than a glorified friendly.

LEFT: A flying Darwin Nunez scores the third goal past Ederson of Manchester City in the FA Community Shield.

before the team would be back in competitive action again in the Community Shield and the clock was already ticking on preparations and plans for another tilt at the title.

Fortunately for Klopp, the summer of 2023 was an unusual one in terms of the global calendar. The anticipated exodus of Liverpool players to the World Cup did not happen after FIFA had finally conceded a tournament June and July in the punishing heat of Qatar was unfeasible, delaying the start of the competition until late November. That meant there would be an unprecedented pre-Christmas break in Premier League proceedings but also more opportunity for the manager to work with a full compliment of players in preseason.

Their travels took the team to Thailand, Singapore, Germany and finally Austria before they returned to the UK at the end of July for the Community Shield showpiece against Manchester City. In another example of the summer's unusual scheduling quirks, the match was played at Leicester City's King Power Stadium rather than Wembley, which was playing host to the final of the Women's Euro 2022 tournament between the Lionesses and Germany the following day.

Given the recent history between Liverpool and City, not least the intense rivalry between Klopp and Guardiola, it was impossible to dismiss the Community Shield as little more than the glorified friendly it had been seen as in previous years. Both managers underlined the importance of the new season's traditional curtain-raiser by selecting the strongest possible starting XI's available to them and as kick-off approached, the two best sides in the country had the chance to lay down an early psychological marker.

The standout name on the Reds' team sheet, albeit on the bench, was Darwin Núñez. A club record £85 million signing from Benfica, the Uruguayan striker had scored 34 goals in 41 games in all competitions for the Portuguese club in 2021-22 and, perhaps even more significantly than his considerable price tag, was the player Klopp had identified as the long-term successor to Sadio Mané. After six scintillating seasons in red and 120 goals, the

Senegalese had left Anfield for Bayern Munich in the summer and the 23-year-old Núñez was the now the heir apparent.

The clash at the King Power was a full-blooded one and 21 minutes into the game Liverpool were in front after Trent Alexander-Arnold curled an effort which took a slight deflection into the far corner of the net. They held their lead for 50 minutes but were pegged back, after a lengthy VAR review, when City scored from close range. By this stage Núñez was already on the pitch, having replaced Roberto Firmino, and the new signing made a match-winning impact. His 83rd-minute header hit a City arm in the area, Mohamed Salah stepping forward to convert the resulting penalty, before the Uruguayan got his own name on the scoresheet with another header deep into injury time.

"Reds supporters have a new hero in Darwin Núñez, who immediately showed what prompted the club to pay Benfica £64m with a debut to remember."

"Reds supporters have a new hero in Darwin Núñez, who immediately showed what prompted the club to pay Benfica £64m with a debut to remember," wrote Shamoon Hafez for *BBC Sport*. "Just 63 days on from that loss in Paris, the Reds were back in action against the side they have formed an intense

but respectful rivalry with over the past four years. The summer signing sealed victory as Liverpool landed the first blow of the season on champions Manchester City by winning a thrilling Community Shield encounter. The FA Cup winners were pipped to the Premier League title by a single point last term after a season-long fight with City, but came out on top in a tremendous game in Leicester. Núñez had the final say, stooping to head in from close range before wheeling off to celebrate in front of his new supporters."

MATCH STATS

THE FA COMMUNITY SHIELD 2022

Saturday, 30 July 2022
(King Power Stadium, Leicester; attendance 28,545)

Liverpool (1) 3 – Manchester City (0) 1
(Alexander-Arnold 21, Salah 83 (pen), Núñez 94) – (Álvarez 70)

Liverpool: Adrián; Alexander-Arnold (Milner 74), Matip, Van Dijk, Robertson, Henderson (Elliott), Fabinho, Thiago (Keïta 85), Salah (Jones 95), Firmino (Núñez 59), Díaz (Carvalho 90).

CHERRY ON THE CAKE

The swashbuckling defeat of City, however, failed to translate into a strong start to the Premier League.

An opening 2-2 draw against Fulham on the banks of the Thames on the opening day of the season was disappointing but not disastrous but when the Reds were held to 1-1 against Crystal Palace at Anfield nine days later, it was clear Liverpool were some distance from their best. What unfolded in their next two fixtures would encapsulate the story of the rest of the side's season domestically and in Europe. The next game at Manchester United came 10 months after Liverpool had stormed to a famous 5-0 victory at Old Trafford but there was no repeat performance in 2022 and their 2-1 defeat left the Reds still in search of their first victory.

The manner in which Klopp's team then banished the dark cloud that hung over them when

ABOVE: Roberto Firmino knocks in number seven for Liverpool in their rout of Bournemouth, August 2022.

Bournemouth were on Merseyside for the fourth game of the campaign was testament to their enduring collective talent and resilient attitude. Any anxiety the home side felt after their uncharacteristic poor run disappeared as early as the third minute when Luis Díaz headed home and when Harvey Elliot registered the first goal of his top-flight career with an unstoppable hit from outside the area three minutes later, the atmosphere at Anfield was as euphoric as ever.

The welcome early breakthrough only made the Reds hungry for more and before the break, Trent Alexander-Arnold added a third. All three had been

Their 9-0 demolition of the Cherries equalled the record for the biggest victory in the history of the Premier League.

assisted by Firmino and the Brazilian then helped himself in the 31st minute, followed by a header from Virgil van Dijk to make it 5-0 as the two teams headed to the dressing rooms. The side could have perhaps been forgiven for easing off the accelerator in the second 45 minutes but when it became six in the first minute after the restart with an own goal, it was obvious there would be no slowing off their pace. Firmino added his second, summer signing Fabio Carvalho opened his Liverpool account for the eighth while Díaz doubled his personal tally five minutes from time to finish the flood of goals.

Their 9-0 demolition of the Cherries equalled the record for the biggest victory in the history of the Premier League. With 19 shots on target in total, it could have been more than nine. Klopp had already described the team's early form as a "false start" and was understandably relieved that the real Liverpool had re-emerged. "We had to prove a point," he admitted. "We had to prove a point for ourselves. I know how it sounds when you lose a game [against Manchester United] and then you try to explain and it's always the same. Each manager in the world is a fantastic entertainer when you win football games. When you have to answer questions when you lose a game you try to find explanations, and obviously they sound like excuses. And that's why the public part of my job is not important, it's just what's the conclusion

ABOVE: Jürgen happily receives a Liverpool top honour, Freedom of the City from the Lord Mayor Roy Gladden.

LEFT: Luis Diaz completes Bournemouth's humiliation with his side's 9th goal.

for us and that's why I said we had to prove a point for us.

"We cannot [always] give guarantees for results, but what we expect from ourselves is that we give guarantees for performance levels and today we started. In the end it was the perfect football afternoon for us, lot of different goalscorers, all these kind of things, wonderful goals, fantastic situations and we know we needed something like that. We had bigger chances in other games and didn't use them. That's the nature of the thing."

Inconsistency however hounded Liverpool through to May. The four matches after the Bournemouth rout yielded only one victory but if there were disappointments, there were also wonderful wins which made even more of a mockery of the Reds mixed results. In October Klopp's side were narrowly beaten at Arsenal but the following weekend welcomed champions City to Merseyside and, for a second time in the season, were victorious over the reigning champions. Full of drama and fiercely contested decisions, the match was settled 14 minutes from the final whistle when Salah latched onto a clearance from Alisson and clinically converted the breakaway chance for the first and only goal at Anfield. There was still time for Klopp to be shown a red card and banished from the touchline late on after his anger boiled over at the referee's decision not to award a free kick after a challenge on Salah but the manager's sending off could not detract from a superb result.

Before the suspension of the Premier League to make way for the World Cup in November – seven of the Reds squad swapped Merseyside for international duty in the Middle East – Klopp received another personal accolade which fondly recognised the remarkable impact he had made in Liverpool since he had left Germany for a new career and life in England. It was the Freedom of the City and in accepting the award at the Town Hall, he became only the second figure after Nelson Mandela born

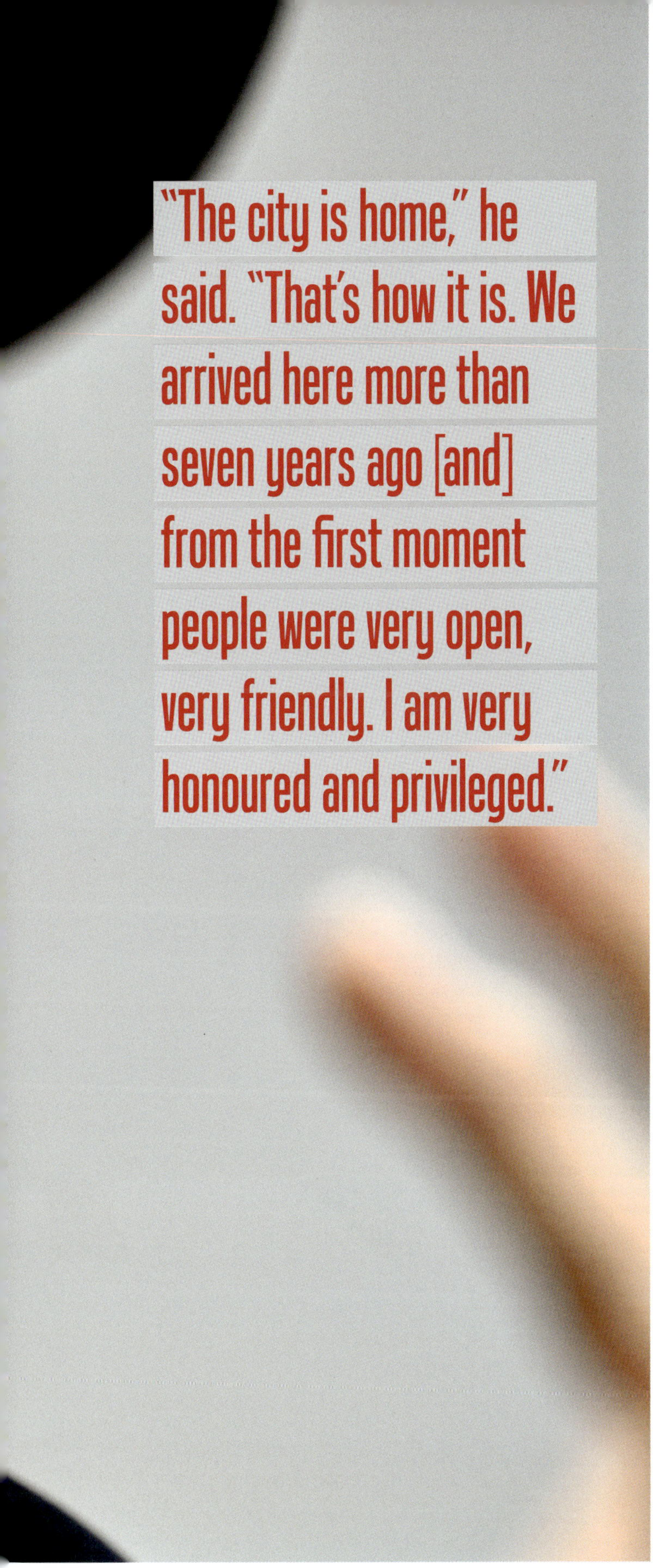

> **"The city is home," he said. "That's how it is. We arrived here more than seven years ago [and] from the first moment people were very open, very friendly. I am very honoured and privileged."**

outside the UK to be honoured in such a way.

"The city is home," he said. "That's how it is. We arrived here more than seven years ago [and] from the first moment people were very open, very friendly. I am very honoured and privileged. One of the duties [of the award] is to defend the city, or in the past it was. I know they meant it differently but I will, with words, forever.

"The Scouse people and us as a family have a lot of things in common. We care about similar things, have similar political views and we like to be very open. I have to be honest, when I first heard this news, I had to take a minute to take it in. As you can imagine, I get a lot of different types of news in my job but this was definitely a 'wow' moment. The main reason for this was what Liverpool, the city and its wonderful people mean to me and my family. The welcome we have been given has been unbelievable, so to get this recognition is incredible. It is also very humbling.

"I am not from Liverpool, so there will be countless people who know [more] about the history than I do, but I actually already knew a little about this award. This was because earlier this year it was granted to Andrew Devine, someone we all had an enormous amount of love for, along with the other 96 victims of Hillsborough."

SEVENTH HEAVEN

Back on the pitch in the New Year, Liverpool's fortunes continued to fluctuate. Already knocked out of the League Cup in December in the fourth round, the Reds survived a replay against Wolves in the third round of the FA Cup, winning 1-0 at Molineux, but were beaten 2-1 at Brighton next time out and with the season at the halfway stage, the team had been dethroned

LEFT: **Jürgen pouring out his soul, in yet another meeting with the media.**

in both domestic cup competitions. There was further knockout football and more heartache in the Champions League. An epic tussle in the group stage, in which Liverpool thrashed Rangers 7-1 in Glasgow, saw Klopp's team finish as runners-up behind Napoli on goal difference and as a result of second place, they faced Real Madrid for a third consecutive season in a repeat of last year's final in Paris.

Revenge was a word Klopp publicly shied away before the Last 16 first leg but it was the only word on the lips of the crowd when the two sides ran out at Anfield. It became a deafening roar after the Reds went two goals up through Núñez and Salah inside the first 14 minutes but the defending

ABOVE: Liverpool visited Dubai in December 2022 for the Super Cup, which they won playing AC Milan.

LEFT: Liverpool's Fabio Carvalho fends off a tackle from Rangers Ryan Jack in their Champions League clash.

champions were level by half time and by the end of a devastating night on Merseyside had completed a 5-2 victory. It was the first time a side had ever scored five at Anfield in a European fixture and when the fairy-tale fightback at the Bernabeu did not happen, Liverpool were out.

There were 16 Premier League matches to play after the team's first leg mauling by Madrid and in early March their hopes of mounting a crucial charge up the table were boosted in record-breaking style after an unforgettable clash with Manchester United at Anfield. Unbeaten in their last four in the league, the Kop was confident ahead of the arrival of their fierce rivals but even the most partisan of Reds supporters could scarcely have believed what they witnessed in 90 minutes of pulsating football.

> **An incisive counterattack saw Salah add the fourth and a second Núñez header made it five.**

It took the home side 43 minutes to break the deadlock. Dutch forward Cody Gakpo, a £37 million January signing from PSV Eindhoven, was the scorer and although his strike was the only score of the first half, it sparked an unstoppable torrent of goals after the restart that destroyed United. Núñez continued the demolition job in the 47th minute while Gakpo doubled his tally three minutes later. An incisive counterattack saw Salah add the fourth and a second Núñez header made it five. An uncharacteristically scrappy finish from Salah gave the Reds six but the manner of the goal was meaningless. His strike took the Egyptian to 129 in the Premier League for the club, eclipsing Robbie Fowler's

"I will find time to re-energise and then we start again."

old record, and it also made the talismanic forward the all-time leading scorer for Liverpool against United with 12. The ecstasy at Anfield then hit fever pitch when Firmino, who had recently announced 2022-23 would be his final season on Merseyside after eight glorious years, netted two minutes from the end to complete a famous 7-0 victory and surpass the club's previous best result against United, a 7-1 thrashing more than 120 years earlier.

"There was rage [in Liverpool] against the dying of the light," wrote Oliver Holt in the *Daily Mail*. Rage that they were being written off and disrespected. Rage that they were being called too old. Rage at the criticism directed at players who have won the Champions League and the Premier League in the last few years and who are not ready to shuffle away to the knacker's yard quite yet. And in 90 minutes of football last night, all that fear, all that rage, all that history between these two clubs came together and burst forth to produce the most astonishing and unexpected result in the history of the titanic clashes between the two most successful clubs in the English game. This 7-0 demolition, this 7-0 humiliation, was the worst defeat United had ever suffered. They had lost 7-0 to Wolves in December 1931, 7-0 to Aston Villa in December 1930 and 7-0 to Blackburn Rovers in April 1926. But none of those defeats came against Liverpool. And losing 7-0 to Liverpool makes this worse. A lot worse."

Inexplicably the dismantling of United was quickly followed by a four-match winless sequence. Momentum however was restored, once again in spectacular style, with a 6-1 win against Leeds United at Elland Road in April. Salah and Diogo Jota both scored twice in West Yorkshire to reignite the season and in their remaining eight games, the Reds were unbeaten. The run included a thrilling 4-3 victory over Tottenham at Anfield which included an injury-time equaliser for the visitors followed seconds later by a Jota winner. But by the time the manager sent out his team for the final fixture of a starkly contrasting campaign against Southampton, the manager knew they could not now break into the top four. The match on the South Coast finished in an entertaining 4-4 draw, confirming a fifth-place finish and the club's place in the Europa League for the following season, and Klopp could reflect on a difficult year. Typically he was the first to acknowledging his side had not met their own sky high expectations but refused to make excuses or accept any suggestion Liverpool would not bounce back.

> "That it didn't turn into the best ever season, we see that, we know that, we are very disappointed about the fact we didn't make it into the top four."

"That it didn't turn into the best ever season, we see that, we know that, we are very disappointed about the fact we didn't make it into the top four," the German said. "There are moments when you have to admit there are four teams that were better than us. That's the truth. If we improve, all of a sudden we are again a team nobody really wants to play against, so that's what we have to become again. I will find time to re-energise and then we start again in July. We played a bad season and we came fifth, that is a message as well. Imagine we are more our normal self, which we absolutely will be again next season, then we will be a contender again."

OPPOSITE: Klopp in celebratory mood after defeating Manchester United at Anfield.

L.F.C.
AXA

THE LAST DANCE (2023-24)

When the new season kicked-off, no one but Jürgen Klopp himself knew it was to be the ninth and final campaign of the German's glittering Anfield reign.

Klopp was leaving with his side in the rudest of health.

Breaking up is hard to do. Especially if one half of the relationship doesn't want it to end. The romance between Klopp and the club, the supporters and the city had only blossomed every year ever since he had arrived on Merseyside in 2015, so when he dramatically revealed 2023-24 would be his swansong season as manager, Liverpool slipped into a state of collective shock. A future without the iconic German on the Anfield touchline was almost impossible to imagine.

It had been only two years earlier that he had signed a new contract to keep him at the club until 2026.

It had been only two years earlier that he had signed a new contract to keep him at the club until 2026. That news was greeted with a joy now only matched by the dismay felt by the Reds faithful. Synonymous with seemingly endless energy and an enduring passion for the game, not to mention Merseyside, it was difficult to believe Klopp had really decided to call it a day.

Liverpool woke up to the surprise announcement in late January with an emotional, personal message from Klopp released by the club. The timing only added to the sense of disbelief, given that it was less than 48 hours after the Reds had booked their place in the League Cup final at Wembley and the team were sitting proudly at the top of the Premier League table. Most managers, whether voluntarily or not, exit in times of crisis and yet Klopp was leaving with his side in the rudest of health and an exciting crop of new signings and rapidly emerging Academy players

LEFT: Fans were left in disbelief at Klopp's unexpected announcement to leave the club.

ABOVE: News had spread in the press about Klopp's imminent departure from Anfield.

to work with as he pressed ahead with what he had called his 'reload' of the squad.

The German of course understood his decision was unexpected and went to great lengths to reassure the fans that he believed he would be betraying them, the players and the club if he blindly saw out the last two years of his contract when he no longer felt he was the best man for the job.

"I can understand that it's a shock for a lot of people in this moment, when you hear it for the first time, but obviously I can explain it, or at least try to explain it," he said. "I love absolutely everything about this club, I love everything about the city, I love everything about our supporters, I love the team, I love the staff. I love everything. But that I still take this decision shows you that I am convinced it is the one I have to take.

"It is that I am, how can I say it, running out of energy. I have no problem now, obviously, I knew it already for longer that I will have to announce it at one point, but I am absolutely fine now. I know that I cannot do the job again and again and again and again. I've been doing this for 24 years. You invest everything you have. I did that and it was never a problem. I realised that my resources are not endless. I preferred to give absolutely everything to this season and then have a break or to stop. We are no young rabbits any more and we don't jump as high as we did.

"This club, especially with the team we have and all the super things we have, needs on top of that a manager in his top game and top level. I cannot be that any more."

"This club, especially with the team we have and all the super things we have, needs on top of that a

"I told the club already in November," he revealed.

manager in his top game and top level. I cannot be that any more. I wish this club for the future the very, very best. I'm convinced it's right. I have no regrets but a lot of special memories. After the years we had together and after all the time we spent together and after all the things we went through together, the respect grew for you, the love grew for you and the least I owe you is the truth – and that is the truth."

Fears that, with six months of the season already gone, the club would now be plunged into a desperate search for a new coach to replace the irreplaceable however we quickly allayed by the German.

"I told the club already in November," he revealed. "I'm on the touchline and in training sessions and stuff like this, but the majority of all the things happen around these kind of things. That means a season starts and you plan pretty much the next season already. When we sat there together talking about potential signings, the next summer camp,

"We are Liverpool, we went through harder things together. And you went through harder things before me. Let's make a strength of it. That would be really cool."

the thought came up, 'I am not sure I am here then anymore' and I was surprised myself by that."

"We are Liverpool, we went through harder things together. And you went through harder things before me. Let's make a strength of it. That would be really cool. Let's squeeze everything out of this season and have another thing to smile about when we look back in the future."

There was one last, weighty question still hanging in the air. Klopp may have been heartbreakingly poised to say goodbye to Anfield but would he ever return to a Premier League touchline wearing his trademark baseball cap with the badge of a rival English club?

"If you ask me 'will you ever work as a manager again?' he said. "I would say now, no. But I don't know obviously how that will feel because I never had the situation. What I know definitely [is that] I will never, ever manage a different club in England than Liverpool. That's not possible. My love for this club, my respect for the people is too big. I couldn't for a second think about it. There's no chance. This is part of my life, we are part of the family."

CHANGING OF THE GUARD

Before Klopp's bombshell in January, the manager and club embarked on what was a significant summer transfer window. The departures of skipper Jordan Henderson, James Milner, Robert Firmino, Fabinho, Alex Oxlade-Chamberlain and Naby Keita in the space of a month represented a major loss of experience and talent but as Klopp was to allude to when he announced his own impending exit, their replacements had already been identified and approached.

Liverpool recruited four new midfielders. Argentine World Cup winner Alexis Mac Allister joined from Brighton for £35 million, rising Hungarian star Dominik Szoboszlai signed in a £60 million deal from RB Leipzig, Japanese Wataru Endō cost £16 million from VfB Stuttgart while Dutch international Ryan Gravenberch was a £34 million buy from Bundesliga giants Bayern Munich. Endō was 30 when he became a Red but their other three new boys were all 24 or younger, signalling Klopp's determination to ensure his eventual successor would not inherit an ageing squad.

The team began their league campaign in considerable style and in their 21 outings between August and January, before the manager made

The match was goalless when Luis Díaz broke clear in the first half.

ABOVE: **Luis Díaz feels the pain of an offside ruling, after scoring against Spurs.**

OPPOSITE: **Bench frustration for Klopp, as some of his finest players are ruled out due to injuries.**

his plan public, they were unbeaten in 20. The only blemish on their record was controversially inflicted in late September in north London when they faced Tottenham. The match was goalless when Luis Díaz broke clear in the first half and scored but his effort was ruled out for offside. VAR confirmed the on-field decision but the refereeing body, the PGMOL, retrospectively admitted human error had returned the wrong verdict. Spurs ran out 2-1 winners at home while Klopp's calls for a replay fell on deaf ears.

The injustice however did little to derail Liverpool's challenge. After they thrashed Luton 4-1 at Anfield in their final league fixture in February, Klopp's side were four points clear at the summit of the table and had scored four goals in no less than six separate matches in the process to underline their attacking prowess.

WEMBLEY FAREWELL

While the Reds made a bold statement of intent in the league, they were no less convincing in League Cup action. The footballing gods were not kind in terms of the draw en route to Wembley – Liverpool faced the Championship leaders and then three fellow Premier League sides – but they met each challenge. Leicester City were despatched 3-1 in the third round before they edged past Bournemouth 2-1 on the south coast courtesy of a second-half

The sense of expectation at Anfield grew.

winner from Darwin Núñez from the bench.

It was altogether more comfortable in the last eight against West Ham, Curtis Jones on target twice in a resounding 5-1 victory at Anfield. Fulham offered sterner resistance in the semi-final but a 1-1 draw in the second leg at Craven Cottage was enough to seal a 3-2 aggregate win and another trip south to London and the home of football.

A Wembley final is never anything but a major occasion but when, two days after the draw at Fulham, it was made public that Klopp was leaving in May, the game assumed an even greater significance and an early opportunity for Liverpool to ensure the German's send-off season was accompanied by silverware. There was a month to wait for the familiar journey to the capital and as each day passed, the sense of expectation at Anfield grew.

The League Cup had given Klopp his first appearance in a final of his Liverpool career back in February 2016. Eight years later, almost to the day, he took his team back to north London and the sense of déjà vu was heightened because Chelsea were once again the opponents. Klopp's side had beaten the Blues twice at Wembley in 2022 in the League and then FA Cup finals and hopes were high the team could make it a hat-trick of triumphs and complete the first leg of a potential, fairy-tale quadruple of trophies.

What was not in the script however was Liverpool's crippling injury list as the match approached. By the time Klopp came to select his 20-strong squad, 11 senior players had been ruled out of contention, including Mohamed Salah, Diogo Jota and Núñez, and the manager had no choice but to trust in youth. That meant 20-year-olds Harvey Elliott and Conor Bradley both started at Wembley while the bench included teenagers Lewis Koumas, Bobby Clark,

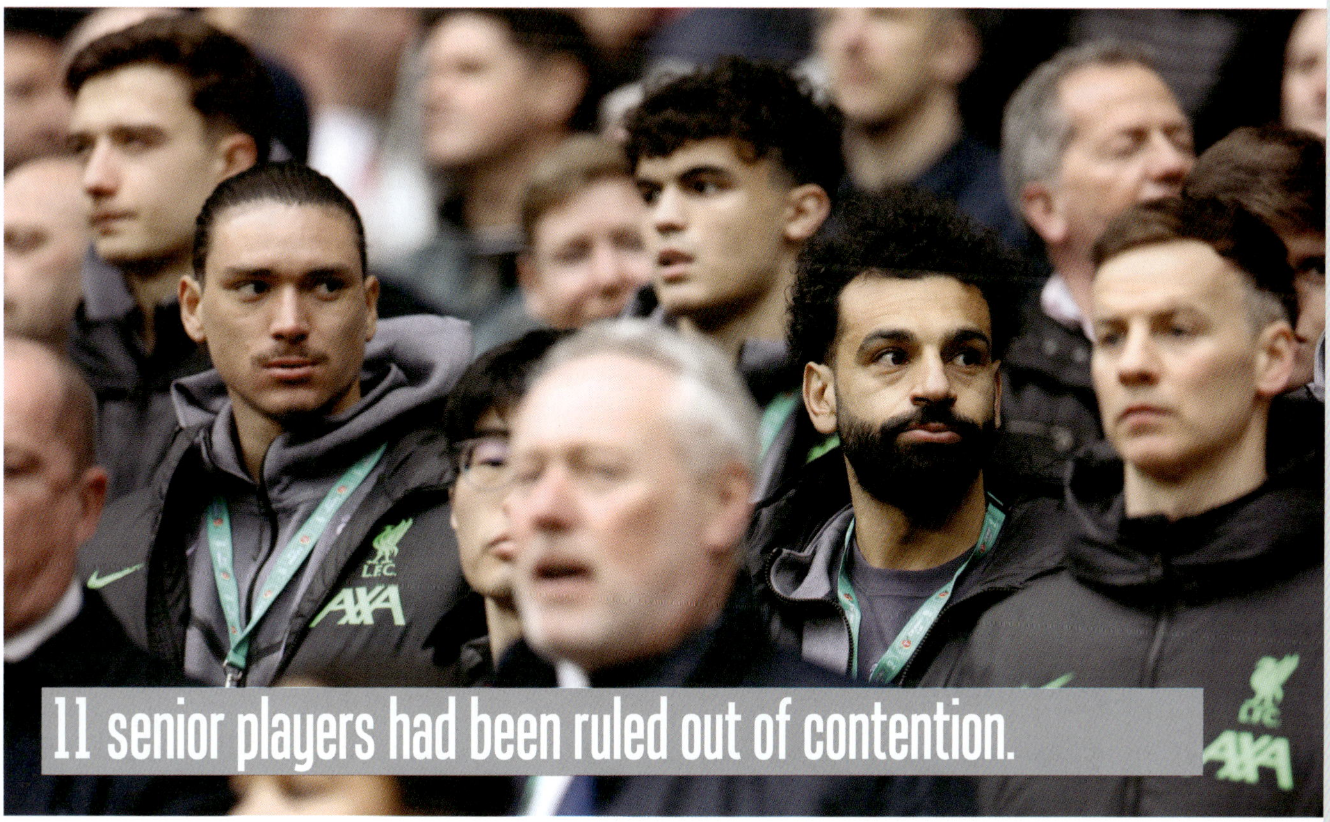

11 senior players had been ruled out of contention.

MATCH STATS

CARABAO CUP FINAL 2024

Sunday, 25 February 2024
(Wembley Stadium, London; attendance 88,868)

Liverpool (0) 1 – Chelsea (0) 0 (aet)
(Van Dijk 118)

Liverpool: Kelleher; Bradley (Clark 72), Konaté (Quansah 106), Robertson (Tsimikas 87), Mac Allister (McConnell 87), Endō, Gravenberch (Gomez 28), Elliott, Gakpo (Danns) 87, Díaz.

Jayden Danns, James McConnell and Trey Nyoni, as well as 21-year-old Jarrell Quansah. The six youthful substitutes boasted just 36 first-team appearances between. Danns had never played a senior game for the club.

The two previous Wembley clashes against Chelsea had been settled by shootouts but this time the lottery of penalties was not required. A tight first half saw Caoimhín Kelleher, the hero of two years ago, brilliantly block Cole Palmer's effort while Cody Gakpo's header for the Reds hit the post. The second period produced a series of chances for both sides as Virgil van Dijk had a goal ruled out for obstruction and Kelleher then denied Conor Gallagher.

By the time the game had reached the nerve-racking second period of extra-time, Klopp had thrust Clark, Quansah, McConnell and Danns into the fray but it was the elder statesman of the team, skipper Van Dijk, who was the match winner when he rose powerfully in the area to head home Kostas Tsimikas' 118th-minute corner. There was no time for Chelsea to respond and Liverpool claim the League Cup for a recording-extending 10th time. Victory gave Klopp his second success in the competition and the seventh

Victory gave Klopp his second success in the competition and the seventh major trophy of his Liverpool career.

ABOVE: The sweet smell of League Cup victory again, as Klopp laps up the attention.

LEFT: Virgil van Dijk scores for the Reds in the Carabao League Cup final against the Blues.

major trophy of his Liverpool career and, just as significantly, it ensured his farewell campaign was one complete with the silverware the players and supporters so desperately wanted to see him lift.

"What happened here was absolutely insane, these things are not possible," the German said after the emotional final whistle. "The team, a squad, an academy full of character. I am so proud I could be part of that. The craziest thing is we deserved it. We had lucky moments, they had lucky moments. The boys showed up, it was really cool."

The celebratory scenes at Wembley spoke volumes about the deep affection for the German but victory also underlined that, even without his infectious presence moving forward, he was leaving Liverpool in a strong position to continue his legacy.

"Liverpool were forced to grit their teeth and fight through pain and adversity, but came up trumps at the end of extra time to beat Chelsea," said the This Is Anfield website. "A tense final 15 minutes ended with, fittingly, a brilliant headed goal from Van Dijk to bring the League Cup back to Anfield. 'The Boss is always directing the spotlight onto his players, but he's quite rightly centre stage today. There was a great Jürgen Klopp Liverpool team that won everything in football. But this isn't that team. This is Liverpool 2.0, Liverpool reloaded, a Liverpool team that will go on without

"It's a Liverpool team that can win trophies."

Klopp in a few months' time. But it's a Liverpool team that can win trophies and they've just ticked off their first."

EUROPEAN RECORD

The dream of a famous quadruple did not materialise. Six unbeaten Premier League outings following the demolition of Luton, including a pulsating 1-1 draw with Manchester City at Anfield in March, ensured it was still a three-horse title race between the Reds, City and Arsenal – just a single point separated the trio of contenders – but April proved Liverpool's Achilles' heel and two wins in the month in their six league fixtures was ultimately the team's undoing.

The clash with City was the 22nd and final time Klopp and Guardiola had crossed swords in all competitions during their respective reigns at Anfield and the Etihad, the German enjoying eight victories in the fixture to seven for the Spaniard. In many ways, both managers' career had been defined by their great rivalry and the mutual respect was evident when the two men embraced at Anfield after the final whistle. "He made us a better team," Guardiola

"He made us a better team," Guardiola said. "He made me a better manager. Football needs personalities like him."

BELOW: Pep Guardiola is only too happy to wish his near rival the best of luck.

OPPOSITE: Klopp knew of the importance of meeting and greeting the endearing Liverpool fans.

Mutual respect was evident when the two men embraced at Anfield.

said. "He made me a better manager. Football needs personalities like him."

Despite April's setbacks, Klopp kept his focus to ensure the Reds safely secured third in the table and Champions League qualification for his successor. The man tasked with filling his shoes was revealed the same month when Liverpool announced 45-year-old Feyenoord manager Arne Slot was the club's choice of replacement and with the succession safely in place, Klopp enjoyed an extended farewell on Merseyside despite characteristically insisting he did not want the end of the season to become about him.

The Reds' FA Cup hopes came to an end in March after a dramatic quarter-final defeat to Manchester United in extra-time at Old Trafford. The side topped their Europa League group before despatching Sparta Prague in the Last 16 with a crushing 11-2 aggregate triumph but the curse of April struck again in the quarter-finals against Italian side Atalanta and they were knocked out. The early rounds of the competition however did give Klopp yet another Liverpool milestone, the 3-1 win away to Austrians LASK in September giving him his 50th win in Europe. The victory saw him surpass Rafa Benítez's previous record of 49 continental victories and become the first Liverpool manager in the club's history to reach a half-century of triumphs.

RIGHT: A sea of banners, flags and scarves at Anfield sends out a defiant message to their manager, as he takes his seat for the last time in a match against Wolves.

JOURNEY'S END

The reluctant assessment of Klopp's Anfield career began the moment he announced his time on Merseyside was coming to an end. The German himself predictably repeatedly refused to discuss where he believed he stood in the distinguished pantheon of Liverpool managers and it was left to others to reflect on his achievements during his nine-year love affair with the club. While many managerial careers are weighed solely in terms of trophies won, it was impossible not to also consider Klopp's wider impact on his adopted city and its people.

Seven major titles with the Reds was testament to his relentless winning mentality.

Seven major titles with the Reds was testament to his relentless winning mentality. His 2024 League Cup triumph elevated Klopp to second in the all-time list of the club's most successful managers above both Bill Shankly and Kenny Dalglish and behind only to Bob Paisley's incredible haul of 14 through the 1970s and '80s. The German's clean sweep of domestic and European honours however outdid Paisley, who never lifted the FA Cup. Shankly did not have a League Cup triumph on his CV while Dalglish never tasted European Cup glory, albeit he was in charge when English sides were banned from UEFA competitions. Klopp's winning rate of 60.9 per cent eclipsed the records of any of the men who had led Liverpool before him.

Comparing Klopp to his fabled predecessors may be subjective but there's little doubt which of his seven successes was the most significant. Liverpool's 30-year wait to be crowned the champions of England for the 19th time was as surprising as it was frustrating but when the title was sealed in 2019-20, the German had achieved the Holy Grail for the club after three decades of disappointment. He could have decamped from Merseyside overnight in the wake of winning the Premier League and still never be forgotten, such was the burning collective desire for the trophy that had painfully eluded the Reds for too long.

The scale of Klopp's achievements can be put

His close relationship with the fans only added to the sincere sense of loss after his departure.

into further context by the club's finances. In his nine seasons in the dugout, Liverpool's net spend on new players was £346 million. That was the lowest of the Premier League's perceived 'Big Six' – Liverpool, the two Manchester clubs, Chelsea, Arsenal and Spurs – and yet the Reds were the second most successful English club between 2015 and 2024. Manchester City invested £1 billion to help secure their trophies over that period while Klopp had worked with, in comparison, a shoestring budget.

His close relationship with the fans only added to the sincere sense of loss after his departure. "He really gets the people of Merseyside," said Margaret Aspinall, a Hillsborough campaigner. "The first time I met him, I was surprised how much knowledge of Hillsborough he had. We've won a lot of things with Jürgen [and] he took our pain away for those 90 minutes. If you only meet him for five seconds, you feel

"You feel as if you've known him for years. I feel he's a Scouser."

as if you've known him for years. I feel he's a Scouser."

The deep affection was echoed by countless other supporters. "He's meant everything to the club," lifelong fan Terry Gerathy told the BBC. "He came in at a time when we were not so good and he's made us great again. He led from the heart but I suppose it was inevitable that he would leave here at some time. I've lived through Shankly, Paisley and he's as close to them as anybody that we've ever had."

It was only in the days leading up to Liverpool's final game of 2023-24, the match against Wolves at Anfield, that Klopp finally allowed himself to reflect on his remarkable journey with the club and the supporters. As disarmingly honest as ever, he admitted the heartbreak of losing the 2022 Champions League final to Real Madrid after the siege of Thibaut Courtois' goal, as well as John Stones' improbable goal line clearance at the Etihad in 2019 that ultimately saw the Reds miss out on the title by a single point, would haunt him.

It was though his affinity with the club, the city of Liverpool and the people that shone through as he looked back over his time on Merseyside. "I'm completely at peace," he said. "It's wonderful to know I spent a big time of my life here. I take fantastic memories with me and friendships forever. The older you get, time slips through your fingers, and you look back and think, that was great. I will not forget a minute or a day of this time. I have met the best people I have ever met and I have worked for the best club I could have imagined in a wonderful, very special city."

Fittingly Klopp's 491st and final game at the helm came at Anfield. Wolves did not upset the party as the Reds ran out 2-0 winners but what unfolded on the pitch was a distant second to the focus on the manager and the club and supporters' long and reluctant goodbye. Anfield was decked with flags declaring 'Jürgen Lives Forever', as well as a banner with the message 'Doubters, Believers, Conquerors',

The break-up was of course painful but the German and the Kop nonetheless parted as lifelong friends.

RIGHT: Following his final game at Anfield, players give Klopp the send off he deserves – forming a guard of honour for their boss.

while the smiling German's walk through a guard of honour after the final whistle was a poignant reminder of the reality that his remarkable tenure was at an end.

Presentations, plaudits and speeches followed but the impact of his reign was more succinctly summed up by the rendition of 'You'll Never Walk Alone' which echoed emotionally around Anfield for the last time with Klopp as manager. The break-up was of course painful but the German and the Kop nonetheless parted as lifelong friends with memories both would treasure in the post-Klopp era.

THANKS FOR THE MEMORIES

Klopp liked nothing better than waving to the Liverpool faithful and of course that uplifting beaming smile was certain to win them over.

There was always time for a laugh and a joke with his players, to relax the atmosphere.

The master at work – touchline anger and emotions were Jürgen's symbol of his dedication to the club.

Klopp takes the lead in Champions League cup-winning celebrations in June 2019.

Behind the scenes post-celebrations, Klopp carries the Premier League trophy in the tunnel at Anfield, July 2020.

Hugs whether you like it or not – Klopp took fan encounters in his stride.

Another pleasing look of sheer elation for Jürgen when Liverpool played host to Sheffield United at Anfield, April 2024.

APPENDIX:
JÜRGEN KLOPP'S LIVERPOOL RECORD

Overall

Played: **491**

Won: **299**

Drawn: **109**

Lost: 83

Goals for: **1035**

Goals against: **503**

Premier League

Played: **334**

Won: **209**

Drawn: **78**

Lost: **47**

FA Cup

Played: **28**

Won: **15**

Drawn: **5**

Lost: **8**

League Cup

Played: **31**

Won: **21**

Drawn: **3**

Lost: **7**

Champions League

Played: **65**

Won: **40**

Drawn: **9**

Lost: **16**

Europa League

Played: **23**

Won: **13**

Drawn: **5**

Lost: **5**

Club Honours

Premier League **2019-20**

FA Cup **2021-22**

League Cup **2021-22, 2023-24**

Champions League **2018-19**

UEFA Super Cup **2019**

FIFA Club World Cup **2019**

Individual Honours

German Football Manager of the Year **2019**

Onze d'Or Coach of the Year **2019**

Best FIFA Men's Coach 2019, **2020**

IFFHS World's Best Club Coach **2019**

IFFHS Men's World Team **2019**

World Soccer World Manager of the Year **2019**

Globe Soccer Best Coach of the Year **2019**

LMA Hall of Fame **2019**

LMA Manager of the Year **2019-20, 2021-22**

Premier League Manager of the Season **2019-20, 2021-22**

Premier League Manager of the Month: September **2016**, December **2018**, March **2019**, August **2019**, September **2019**, November **2019**, December **2019**, January **2020**, May **2021**, January **2024**

BBC Sports Personality of the Year Coach Award **2020**

STADIUM TOURS